50 Japan Spring Season Recipes for Home

By: Kelly Johnson

Table of Contents

- Sakura Mochi
- Shiso Leaf Tempura
- Cherry Blossom Rice
- Takoyaki (Octopus Balls)
- Asparagus Tempura
- Bamboo Shoot Salad
- Hanami Dango (Flower Viewing Skewers)
- Umeboshi Rice Balls
- Spring Roll with Shrimp and Vegetables
- Spinach and Sesame Salad
- Miso-Glazed Eggplant
- Japanese Chilled Tofu
- Soba Noodle Salad
- Grilled Salmon with Teriyaki Glaze
- Sweet Pea and Shrimp Tempura
- Green Tea Ice Cream
- Fresh Edamame Beans
- Japanese Cucumber Salad
- Udon Noodles in a Light Broth
- Smoked Salmon and Avocado Sushi
- Japanese Chive Pancakes (Negi Yaki)
- Cold Soba with Dipping Sauce
- Soft-Boiled Egg with Soy Sauce
- Lotus Root and Carrot Stir-Fry
- Shoyu Ramen with Spring Vegetables
- Pickled Cherry Blossoms
- Daikon Radish Salad
- Japanese Potato Salad
- Tofu and Vegetable Stir-Fry
- Miso Soup with Asparagus
- Sweet Potato Tempura
- Sushi Rolls with Seasonal Vegetables

- Chilled Japanese Noodle Salad (Hiyashi Chuka)
- Radish and Cucumber Pickles
- Spicy Tuna Tartare
- Green Tea Mochi
- Japanese Spring Vegetable Curry
- Spinach Goma-ae (Spinach with Sesame Dressing)
- Strawberry Daifuku
- Teriyaki Chicken with Seasonal Vegetables
- Miso-Glazed Grilled Eggplant
- Japanese Style Pancakes (Okonomiyaki)
- Chilled Edamame Salad
- Shrimp and Vegetable Tempura
- Japanese Beef and Vegetable Skewers (Kushikatsu)
- Sweet Corn and Shrimp Croquettes
- Grilled Asparagus with Soy Sauce
- Japanese Sweet Potato and Chestnut Soup
- Cherry Blossom Cake
- Matcha Green Tea Cheesecake

Sakura Mochi

Ingredients:

For the Mochi:

- **1 cup sweet rice flour** (also known as mochiko or glutinous rice flour)
- **1 cup water**
- **1/2 cup sugar**
- **1/2 teaspoon salt**

For the Filling:

- **1/2 cup red bean paste** (anko, preferably smooth)
- **1 tablespoon sugar** (optional, adjust to taste)

For Wrapping:

- **12-15 pickled cherry blossom leaves** (sakura no ha), soaked in water to remove excess salt and then dried

Instructions:

1. Prepare the Filling:

- **Make Filling:** If using store-bought red bean paste, you can adjust the sweetness by mixing it with a bit of sugar if desired. Divide the red bean paste into 12-15 small balls, about 1 tablespoon each. Set aside.

2. Make the Mochi Dough:

- **Mix Ingredients:** In a heatproof bowl, mix the sweet rice flour, sugar, and salt. Gradually add the water and stir until the mixture is smooth and free of lumps.
- **Cook Mochi:** Steam the mixture in a steamer lined with parchment paper or a heatproof cloth for about 20-25 minutes, or until it becomes translucent and firm. Stir occasionally to ensure even cooking.

3. Shape the Mochi:

- **Cool the Dough:** Let the steamed dough cool slightly until it's manageable, but still warm.
- **Divide Dough:** Dust your hands or work surface with cornstarch or potato starch to prevent sticking. Divide the dough into 12-15 pieces.
- **Form Mochi:** Flatten each piece of dough into a round disk, place a red bean paste ball in the center, and wrap the dough around the filling, pinching the edges together to seal. Roll into a smooth ball.

4. Wrap with Cherry Blossom Leaves:

- **Prepare Leaves:** If the cherry blossom leaves are too salty, soak them in water for a few hours, then rinse and pat dry.
- **Wrap Mochi:** Wrap each mochi ball with a pickled cherry blossom leaf. The leaf adds flavor and fragrance to the mochi.

5. Serve:

- **Presentation:** Place the wrapped sakura mochi on a serving plate. You can serve them immediately or let them sit for a few hours for the flavors to meld.

Tips:

- **Pickled Cherry Blossom Leaves:** These leaves are available in Asian grocery stores or online. They are often salted and preserved, giving the mochi its unique aroma. If you can't find them, you can skip the wrapping, though it won't have the traditional flavor.
- **Handling Mochi:** Sweet rice dough can be sticky. Dusting with cornstarch or potato starch helps prevent sticking.
- **Sweet Red Bean Paste:** You can adjust the sweetness of the red bean paste based on your preference.

Enjoy your homemade Sakura Mochi as a beautiful and delicious treat that celebrates the cherry blossom season!

Shiso Leaf Tempura

Ingredients:

- **15-20 fresh shiso leaves** (washed and dried)
- **1 cup all-purpose flour**
- **1/2 cup cornstarch**
- **1 teaspoon baking powder**
- **1/2 teaspoon salt**
- **1 cup ice-cold sparkling water** (or cold water)
- **1 large egg** (optional, for a richer batter)
- **Vegetable oil** (for frying, such as canola or sunflower oil)
- **Sea salt** (for sprinkling, optional)

Instructions:

1. Prepare the Batter:

- **Mix Dry Ingredients:** In a bowl, combine the flour, cornstarch, baking powder, and salt.
- **Add Wet Ingredients:** In another bowl, lightly beat the egg (if using) and then add it to the dry ingredients. Gradually mix in the ice-cold sparkling water (or cold water) until just combined. The batter should be lumpy; do not overmix.

2. Heat the Oil:

- **Prepare Oil:** In a deep skillet or pot, heat about 2 inches of vegetable oil to 350°F (175°C). Use a thermometer to check the temperature. If you don't have a thermometer, test the oil by dropping a small amount of batter into it; it should sizzle and rise to the surface.

3. Batter the Shiso Leaves:

- **Dip Leaves:** Holding a shiso leaf by the stem, dip it into the tempura batter, ensuring it's coated evenly. Allow excess batter to drip off.

4. Fry the Shiso Leaves:

- **Fry in Batches:** Carefully place the battered shiso leaves into the hot oil. Fry in batches to avoid overcrowding, which can lower the oil temperature and result in greasy tempura.
- **Cook Until Crisp:** Fry for about 1-2 minutes or until the batter is golden and crispy. Flip the leaves halfway through cooking for even browning.
- **Drain:** Use a slotted spoon to remove the tempura leaves from the oil and drain on a plate lined with paper towels.

5. Serve:

- **Garnish and Enjoy:** Sprinkle the tempura shiso leaves with a little sea salt if desired. Serve warm as an appetizer or side dish.

Tips:

- **Cold Batter:** Keeping the batter cold helps achieve a light, crispy texture. If the batter warms up, it may become heavy and less crispy.
- **Oil Temperature:** Maintaining the correct oil temperature is crucial for crispy tempura. If the oil is too hot, the batter may burn; if it's too cool, the tempura will be greasy.
- **Shiso Leaves:** Make sure the shiso leaves are dry before dipping them in the batter to prevent excess oil splatter.

Enjoy your Shiso Leaf Tempura as a crispy and flavorful treat that highlights the unique taste of shiso leaves!

Cherry Blossom Rice

Ingredients:

- **2 cups short-grain or sushi rice**
- **2 1/2 cups water** (or according to rice package instructions)
- **1 tablespoon sake** (Japanese rice wine)
- **1 tablespoon soy sauce** (optional, for a touch of umami)
- **10-15 pickled cherry blossoms** (sakura no ha), soaked in water to remove excess salt, then drained
- **1 tablespoon sakura-flavored salt** (optional, for enhanced cherry blossom flavor)
- **1 tablespoon sugar** (optional, to balance the saltiness)
- **1 sheet nori** (seaweed), cut into thin strips (for garnish, optional)
- **Chopped green onions** (for garnish, optional)

Instructions:

1. Prepare the Rice:

- **Rinse Rice:** Rinse the rice under cold water until the water runs clear. This removes excess starch and helps prevent the rice from becoming gummy.
- **Cook Rice:** Combine the rinsed rice and water in a rice cooker. Add the sake and soy sauce if using. Cook according to the rice cooker's instructions. If using a pot, bring to a boil, then reduce heat to low, cover, and simmer for about 15-20 minutes until the water is absorbed and the rice is tender.

2. Prepare the Pickled Cherry Blossoms:

- **Soak Blossoms:** If the pickled cherry blossoms are very salty, soak them in water for a few hours to remove excess salt. After soaking, gently pat them dry with a paper towel.

3. Mix Cherry Blossoms with Rice:

- **Cool Rice:** Once the rice is cooked, let it cool slightly before mixing.
- **Fold in Blossoms:** Gently fold the pickled cherry blossoms into the cooked rice. If desired, you can also add a bit of sakura-flavored salt and sugar to enhance the flavor. Be careful not to overmix to avoid breaking the blossoms.

4. Garnish and Serve:

- **Garnish:** Transfer the cherry blossom rice to a serving dish. Garnish with nori strips and chopped green onions if desired.
- **Serve:** Serve warm or at room temperature as a side dish or main component of your meal.

Tips:

- **Pickled Cherry Blossoms:** You can find pickled cherry blossoms in Asian grocery stores or online. If unavailable, you can use dried sakura flowers, but they should be rehydrated before use.
- **Rice Variations:** You can adjust the amount of pickled cherry blossoms based on your taste preference. Some might prefer a stronger floral flavor, while others may want just a hint.
- **Flavor Adjustments:** If the rice is too salty or too bland, adjust with a bit more sugar or salt to balance the flavors.

Enjoy your Cherry Blossom Rice as a beautiful and flavorful way to celebrate the cherry blossom season!

Takoyaki (Octopus Balls)

Ingredients:

For the Takoyaki Batter:

- 1 cup all-purpose flour
- 1 tablespoon cornstarch
- 1/2 teaspoon baking powder
- 1/2 teaspoon salt
- 2 large eggs
- 1 1/2 cups dashi stock (or water)
- 2 tablespoons soy sauce
- 1 tablespoon mirin (sweet rice wine)

For the Filling:

- **1/2 cup cooked octopus**, chopped into small pieces (you can use fresh, boiled octopus or pre-cooked)
- **1/4 cup pickled ginger**, finely chopped
- **1/4 cup green onions**, finely chopped
- **1/4 cup tempura bits** (tenkasu, optional, for added crunch)
- **1/4 cup shredded cheese** (optional, for a richer taste)

For Topping:

- **Takoyaki sauce** (store-bought or homemade)
- **Japanese mayonnaise**
- **Bonito flakes** (katsuobushi)
- **Dried seaweed flakes** (aonori)
- **Chopped green onions**

Equipment:

- **Takoyaki pan** (a special pan with small round molds)

Instructions:

1. Prepare the Batter:

- **Mix Dry Ingredients:** In a large bowl, whisk together the flour, cornstarch, baking powder, and salt.
- **Add Wet Ingredients:** In another bowl, beat the eggs and then add the dashi stock, soy sauce, and mirin. Mix well.
- **Combine:** Gradually pour the wet mixture into the dry ingredients, stirring until just combined. The batter should be smooth and somewhat runny.

2. Preheat the Takoyaki Pan:

- **Heat Pan:** Place the takoyaki pan on medium heat and lightly oil the molds using a brush or paper towel. Allow the pan to heat up for a few minutes.

3. Cook the Takoyaki:

- **Fill Molds:** Pour the batter into each mold, filling them about 3/4 full.
- **Add Filling:** Place a few pieces of octopus, pickled ginger, green onions, tempura bits, and cheese (if using) into each mold.
- **Cook and Flip:** Cook for about 2-3 minutes until the batter starts to set. Using a takoyaki pick or chopsticks, gently turn each ball by 90 degrees to cook all sides evenly. Continue cooking and turning until the takoyaki balls are golden brown and crispy on the outside, about 5-7 minutes total.

4. Serve:

- **Remove Takoyaki:** Use a pick or chopsticks to carefully remove the takoyaki balls from the pan.
- **Add Toppings:** Place the takoyaki on a serving plate. Drizzle with takoyaki sauce and Japanese mayonnaise. Sprinkle with bonito flakes, dried seaweed flakes, and chopped green onions.

Tips:

- **Octopus Preparation:** If using fresh octopus, make sure it is cooked thoroughly. Boiling it until tender is usually best. Pre-cooked octopus is also available in many Asian grocery stores.
- **Takoyaki Pan:** If you don't have a takoyaki pan, you can use a regular non-stick pan or even a muffin tin, but the results will differ slightly.
- **Batter Consistency:** The batter should be somewhat runny to fill the molds and cook properly. If it's too thick, add a bit more dashi or water.

Enjoy your homemade Takoyaki as a fun and tasty Japanese treat!

Asparagus Tempura

Ingredients:

For the Tempura Batter:

- 1 cup all-purpose flour
- 1/2 cup cornstarch
- 1 teaspoon baking powder
- 1/2 teaspoon salt
- 1 cup ice-cold sparkling water (or cold water)
- 1 large egg (optional, for extra crispiness)

For the Asparagus:

- 12-15 fresh asparagus spears
- Vegetable oil (for frying, such as canola or sunflower oil)

For Serving:

- Tempura dipping sauce (tentsuyu)
- Shredded daikon radish (optional, for garnish)
- Chopped green onions (optional, for garnish)
- Grated ginger (optional, for garnish)

Instructions:

1. Prepare the Asparagus:

- **Trim Asparagus:** Wash and trim the woody ends of the asparagus. You can leave them whole or cut them into shorter lengths if desired.

2. Make the Tempura Batter:

- **Mix Dry Ingredients:** In a bowl, combine the flour, cornstarch, baking powder, and salt.
- **Add Wet Ingredients:** In a separate bowl, lightly beat the egg (if using) and then add it to the dry ingredients. Gradually mix in the ice-cold sparkling water (or cold water) until just combined. The batter should be lumpy; do not overmix.

3. Heat the Oil:

- **Prepare Oil:** In a deep skillet or pot, heat about 2 inches of vegetable oil to 350°F (175°C). Use a thermometer to check the temperature. If you don't have a thermometer, test the oil by dropping a small amount of batter into it; it should sizzle and rise to the surface.

4. Coat and Fry the Asparagus:

- **Coat Asparagus:** Dip each asparagus spear into the tempura batter, allowing excess batter to drip off.
- **Fry in Batches:** Carefully place the battered asparagus into the hot oil. Fry in batches to avoid overcrowding, which can lower the oil temperature and result in greasy tempura.
- **Cook Until Crisp:** Fry for about 2-4 minutes, or until the batter is golden brown and crispy. Flip the asparagus halfway through cooking for even browning.
- **Drain:** Use a slotted spoon to remove the tempura from the oil and drain on a plate lined with paper towels.

5. Serve:

- **Garnish and Enjoy:** Serve the asparagus tempura warm with tempura dipping sauce on the side. You can also garnish with shredded daikon radish, chopped green onions, and grated ginger if desired.

Tips:

- **Cold Batter:** Keeping the batter cold is key to achieving a light and crispy texture. The ice-cold sparkling water helps make the batter crisp.
- **Oil Temperature:** Maintaining a consistent oil temperature is crucial for crispy tempura. If the oil temperature drops too low, the tempura may become greasy.
- **Batter Variations:** You can experiment with the batter by adding a pinch of spices or seasoning for extra flavor.

Enjoy your crispy and delicious Asparagus Tempura!

Bamboo Shoot Salad

Ingredients:

- **1 can or 1 cup fresh bamboo shoots**, sliced thinly (if using fresh, peel and slice them)
- **1 medium carrot**, julienned or sliced thinly
- **1 cucumber**, julienned or sliced thinly
- **1/4 cup fresh cilantro** (or shiso leaves), chopped
- **1/4 cup sesame seeds**, toasted
- **2 tablespoons rice vinegar**
- **1 tablespoon soy sauce**
- **1 tablespoon sesame oil**
- **1 teaspoon sugar**
- **1 teaspoon grated ginger** (optional)
- **1 small red chili**, sliced thinly (optional, for a touch of heat)

Instructions:

1. Prepare the Bamboo Shoots:

- **If Using Canned Bamboo Shoots:** Rinse the bamboo shoots under cold water to remove excess sodium. Drain and slice thinly.
- **If Using Fresh Bamboo Shoots:** Peel the bamboo shoots and slice them thinly. Boil in salted water for about 15-20 minutes until tender. Drain and cool before using.

2. Prepare the Vegetables:

- **Carrots and Cucumber:** Julienne or slice the carrot and cucumber thinly. You can use a mandoline for uniform slices.

3. Make the Dressing:

- **Combine Ingredients:** In a small bowl, whisk together the rice vinegar, soy sauce, sesame oil, sugar, and grated ginger (if using) until the sugar is dissolved and the dressing is well combined.

4. Assemble the Salad:

- **Mix Vegetables:** In a large bowl, combine the bamboo shoots, carrot, and cucumber.
- **Add Dressing:** Pour the dressing over the vegetables and toss gently to coat everything evenly.

5. Garnish and Serve:

- **Add Garnishes:** Sprinkle with toasted sesame seeds and fresh cilantro (or shiso leaves). Add sliced red chili if desired for a touch of heat.

- **Serve:** Serve the salad immediately, or let it chill in the refrigerator for about 30 minutes to allow the flavors to meld.

Tips:

- **Fresh Bamboo Shoots:** If using fresh bamboo shoots, make sure they are properly cooked and tender before adding them to the salad.
- **Adjust Seasoning:** Taste the dressing and adjust the seasoning according to your preference. You can add more soy sauce for saltiness or more sugar for sweetness.
- **Texture:** For added crunch, you can add other vegetables like bell peppers or radishes.

This Bamboo Shoot Salad is a light and flavorful dish perfect for springtime or any time you're looking for a refreshing and crisp salad. Enjoy!

Hanami Dango (Flower Viewing Skewers)

Ingredients:

For the Dango:

- **1 cup sweet rice flour** (mochiko or glutinous rice flour)
- **1/2 cup sugar**
- **1/2 cup water** (adjust as needed)
- **Red and green food coloring** (or matcha powder for green, and pink food coloring or beet juice for pink)
- **1/4 cup cornstarch or potato starch** (for dusting)

For the Skewers:

- **Wooden skewers** (pre-soaked in water to prevent burning during grilling)

Instructions:

1. Prepare the Dango Mixture:

- **Mix Dry Ingredients:** In a bowl, combine the sweet rice flour and sugar.
- **Add Water:** Gradually add water to the dry ingredients while stirring until the mixture is smooth and slightly thick. The consistency should be like a thick batter, not too runny.

2. Divide and Color the Dough:

- **Divide Dough:** Divide the dough into three equal parts.
- **Color Dough:** Add a few drops of red food coloring to one part of the dough to make it pink. Mix until well combined. Add green food coloring or matcha powder to another part to make it green. Leave the remaining dough white.

3. Shape the Dango:

- **Form Balls:** Dust your hands with cornstarch or potato starch. Take a small amount of each colored dough and roll it into a ball about 1 inch in diameter.
- **Assemble Skewers:** Thread the colored dango balls onto the wooden skewers, alternating colors for a festive look. Usually, each skewer has 3-4 dango balls.

4. Cook the Dango:

- **Boil:** Bring a large pot of water to a boil. Carefully drop the skewers with dango balls into the boiling water. Boil for about 2-3 minutes or until the dango float to the surface and become slightly translucent.
- **Cool:** Remove the skewers from the water and let them cool on a plate.

5. Grill (Optional):

- **Grill for Additional Flavor:** If desired, lightly grill the dango skewers over an open flame or a grill pan for a few minutes to give them a slightly smoky flavor. This step is optional but adds a nice touch.

6. Serve:

- **Presentation:** Serve the Hanami Dango skewers as a sweet treat during a cherry blossom viewing party or any time you want to enjoy a colorful and festive Japanese dessert.

Tips:

- **Dango Consistency:** If the dough is too sticky, add a bit more sweet rice flour. If it's too dry, add a little more water.
- **Color Variations:** You can use different colors for a more vibrant presentation or even use natural colors like beet juice for pink and matcha for green.
- **Storage:** Hanami Dango is best enjoyed fresh but can be stored in an airtight container for a day or two.

Enjoy your Hanami Dango as a delightful and colorful treat, perfect for celebrating the cherry blossom season!

Umeboshi Rice Balls

Ingredients:

- **2 cups short-grain or sushi rice**
- **2 1/2 cups water** (or according to rice package instructions)
- **5-6 umeboshi plums** (pickled plums)
- **1 tablespoon sesame seeds** (optional, for garnish)
- **Nori (seaweed) sheets**, cut into strips (optional, for wrapping)
- **Salt** (for seasoning)

Instructions:

1. Prepare the Rice:

- **Rinse Rice:** Rinse the rice under cold water until the water runs clear to remove excess starch. This helps prevent the rice from becoming too sticky.
- **Cook Rice:** Combine the rinsed rice and water in a rice cooker. Cook according to the rice cooker's instructions. If using a pot, bring the rice and water to a boil, then reduce heat to low, cover, and simmer for about 15-20 minutes until the water is absorbed and the rice is tender. Let the rice sit for 10 minutes, then fluff with a fork.

2. Prepare Umeboshi:

- **Pit Umeboshi:** Remove the pits from the umeboshi plums. You can do this by gently pressing them to expose the pit and then discarding it.
- **Mash or Chop:** Mash the umeboshi plums into a paste using a fork or chop them finely. If the umeboshi is too salty or strong for your taste, you can mix it with a little bit of sugar or honey to balance the flavor.

3. Shape the Rice Balls:

- **Cool Rice:** Let the cooked rice cool slightly until it is comfortable to handle.
- **Season Rice:** Lightly season the rice with a bit of salt to taste.
- **Form Balls:** Wet your hands with water to prevent sticking. Take a small amount of rice (about 1/4 cup) and flatten it into a small disk. Place a small spoonful of umeboshi paste in the center of the rice. Gently fold the edges of the rice around the filling and shape the rice into a ball or triangle, sealing the umeboshi inside.

4. Wrap with Nori (Optional):

- **Wrap:** If using nori, cut the sheets into strips and wrap them around the rice balls. This adds a nice texture and additional flavor.

5. Garnish and Serve:

- **Garnish:** Sprinkle the rice balls with toasted sesame seeds if desired.
- **Serve:** Serve the umeboshi rice balls at room temperature or slightly warm. They are great as a snack, lunch, or picnic item.

Tips:

- **Rice Consistency:** The rice should be slightly sticky to hold its shape well. If the rice is too dry, it might not form well.
- **Umeboshi Paste:** If you find umeboshi too strong, try blending it with a little bit of honey or sugar to soften the flavor.
- **Storage:** Umeboshi rice balls are best eaten fresh but can be stored in an airtight container at room temperature for up to a day. They can also be refrigerated for a couple of days.

Enjoy your Umeboshi Rice Balls as a delicious and traditional Japanese treat!

Spring Roll with Shrimp and Vegetables

Ingredients:

For the Spring Rolls:

- **1/2 pound shrimp**, peeled, deveined, and chopped
- **1 cup shredded carrots**
- **1 cup shredded cabbage** (green or Napa cabbage)
- **1/2 cup bean sprouts**
- **1/4 cup thinly sliced green onions**
- **1/4 cup fresh cilantro**, chopped
- **1 tablespoon soy sauce**
- **1 teaspoon sesame oil**
- **1/2 teaspoon minced garlic**
- **1/2 teaspoon minced ginger**
- **Spring roll wrappers** (store-bought, usually found in Asian grocery stores)

For Frying:

- **Vegetable oil** (for frying, such as canola or sunflower oil)

For Dipping Sauce:

- **1/4 cup soy sauce**
- **1 tablespoon rice vinegar**
- **1 tablespoon sugar**
- **1 teaspoon sesame oil**
- **1 teaspoon chili sauce** (optional, for heat)

Instructions:

1. Prepare the Filling:

- **Cook Shrimp:** In a pan over medium heat, add a small amount of oil. Cook the shrimp until pink and opaque, about 2-3 minutes per side. Remove from heat and let cool slightly. Chop into small pieces.
- **Stir-Fry Vegetables:** In the same pan, add a little oil if needed. Stir-fry the shredded carrots, shredded cabbage, bean sprouts, garlic, and ginger until tender, about 3-4 minutes. Season with soy sauce and sesame oil. Remove from heat and let cool.
- **Combine Filling:** In a large bowl, combine the chopped shrimp, stir-fried vegetables, green onions, and cilantro. Mix well.

2. Assemble the Spring Rolls:

- **Prepare Wrappers:** Follow the instructions on the spring roll wrappers package. Usually, you need to soften the wrappers by dipping them in warm water for a few seconds until pliable.
- **Fill and Roll:** Lay a softened wrapper on a clean surface. Place a small amount of the filling in the center of the wrapper. Fold the sides over the filling, then roll from the bottom to form a tight cylinder. Seal the edge with a little water if needed.

3. Fry the Spring Rolls:

- **Heat Oil:** In a deep skillet or pot, heat about 2 inches of vegetable oil to 350°F (175°C). Use a thermometer to check the temperature. If you don't have a thermometer, test the oil by dropping a small piece of bread into it; it should sizzle and turn golden.
- **Fry in Batches:** Carefully add the spring rolls to the hot oil, a few at a time, without overcrowding. Fry for 3-4 minutes, turning occasionally, until golden brown and crispy.
- **Drain:** Use a slotted spoon to remove the spring rolls from the oil and drain on a plate lined with paper towels.

4. Prepare the Dipping Sauce:

- **Mix Ingredients:** In a small bowl, combine the soy sauce, rice vinegar, sugar, sesame oil, and chili sauce (if using). Stir until the sugar is dissolved.

5. Serve:

- **Presentation:** Serve the spring rolls hot, with the dipping sauce on the side. You can also garnish with extra cilantro or sliced green onions if desired.

Tips:

- **Wrapping:** Make sure the spring roll wrappers are not too wet before filling to avoid them becoming too sticky or tearing.
- **Frying:** Ensure the oil is hot enough before frying to achieve a crispy texture. If the oil is too cool, the spring rolls can become greasy.
- **Variation:** Feel free to add other vegetables or proteins to the filling based on your preference.

Enjoy your homemade Shrimp and Vegetable Spring Rolls with a flavorful dipping sauce!

Spinach and Sesame Salad

Ingredients:

- **6 cups fresh spinach leaves**, washed and dried
- **1/4 cup sesame seeds**, toasted
- **1/4 cup sliced almonds** (optional, for extra crunch)
- **1/4 cup soy sauce**
- **2 tablespoons rice vinegar**
- **1 tablespoon sesame oil**
- **1 tablespoon honey** or **sugar** (adjust to taste)
- **1 teaspoon grated ginger**
- **1 clove garlic**, minced
- **1 tablespoon chopped green onions** (optional, for garnish)
- **1 teaspoon sesame seeds**, for garnish (optional)

Instructions:

1. Toast the Sesame Seeds:

- **Heat Pan:** In a dry skillet over medium heat, add the sesame seeds. Toast, stirring frequently, until they turn golden brown and become fragrant. This should take about 2-3 minutes. Be careful not to burn them. Remove from heat and set aside.

2. Prepare the Dressing:

- **Combine Ingredients:** In a small bowl or jar, whisk together the soy sauce, rice vinegar, sesame oil, honey (or sugar), grated ginger, and minced garlic until well combined. Taste and adjust seasoning if needed. If you prefer a sweeter or tangier dressing, adjust the honey or vinegar accordingly.

3. Assemble the Salad:

- **Combine Spinach and Nuts:** In a large salad bowl, combine the fresh spinach leaves with the toasted sesame seeds. If using, add the sliced almonds for extra crunch.
- **Dress the Salad:** Drizzle the prepared dressing over the spinach mixture. Toss gently to coat the spinach evenly with the dressing.

4. Garnish and Serve:

- **Garnish:** Sprinkle with additional sesame seeds and chopped green onions if desired.
- **Serve:** Serve immediately for the freshest taste.

Tips:

- **Toast Sesame Seeds:** Toasting the sesame seeds enhances their flavor and crunch. If you prefer, you can also use black sesame seeds for a more intense flavor and color contrast.
- **Variations:** You can add other ingredients to the salad, such as sliced cucumbers, shredded carrots, or radishes for added texture and flavor.
- **Make Ahead:** If making ahead, keep the dressing separate and add it just before serving to prevent the spinach from wilting.

This Spinach and Sesame Salad is a versatile and tasty addition to any meal, providing a nutritious and flavorful option that's easy to prepare. Enjoy!

Miso-Glazed Eggplant

Ingredients:

- **2 medium eggplants** (Japanese or Chinese eggplants work well, but regular eggplants are fine too)
- **2 tablespoons miso paste** (white or red miso, depending on your preference)
- **2 tablespoons mirin** (sweet rice wine)
- **1 tablespoon soy sauce**
- **1 tablespoon sugar** (adjust to taste)
- **1 tablespoon sesame oil**
- **1 teaspoon grated ginger** (optional)
- **1-2 cloves garlic**, minced (optional)
- **Sesame seeds** (for garnish)
- **Chopped green onions** (for garnish)

Instructions:

1. Prepare the Eggplant:

- **Slice Eggplant:** Cut the eggplants in half lengthwise. If using larger eggplants, you might want to cut them into quarters.
- **Score the Flesh:** Using a knife, score the flesh of each eggplant half in a crisscross pattern. This helps the miso glaze penetrate and ensures even cooking.

2. Make the Miso Glaze:

- **Combine Ingredients:** In a small bowl, mix together the miso paste, mirin, soy sauce, sugar, sesame oil, grated ginger (if using), and minced garlic (if using) until smooth and well combined.

3. Apply the Glaze:

- **Coat Eggplant:** Brush or spoon the miso glaze evenly over the cut sides of the eggplants. Make sure to get some of the glaze into the scored cuts for maximum flavor.

4. Cook the Eggplant:

- **Roasting Method:**
  - **Preheat Oven:** Preheat your oven to 400°F (200°C).
  - **Roast Eggplant:** Place the glazed eggplants cut-side up on a baking sheet lined with parchment paper. Roast for 20-25 minutes, or until the eggplants are tender and the glaze is caramelized.
- **Grilling Method:**
  - **Preheat Grill:** Preheat your grill to medium heat.

- **Grill Eggplant:** Place the glazed eggplants cut-side down on the grill. Grill for 4-5 minutes until grill marks appear, then flip and grill for an additional 4-5 minutes, or until the eggplants are tender and the glaze is caramelized.

5. Garnish and Serve:

- **Garnish:** Sprinkle the roasted or grilled eggplants with sesame seeds and chopped green onions.
- **Serve:** Serve warm as a side dish or over rice as a main course.

Tips:

- **Eggplant Preparation:** If you want to reduce the bitterness of eggplant, you can salt the slices before cooking. Sprinkle salt on the cut sides, let them sit for 30 minutes, then rinse and pat dry before applying the glaze.
- **Glaze Variations:** You can adjust the sweetness or saltiness of the glaze by varying the amount of sugar or soy sauce according to your taste.
- **Serving Suggestions:** Miso-glazed eggplant pairs well with steamed rice and can be enjoyed alongside other Japanese dishes like miso soup or teriyaki chicken.

Enjoy your Miso-Glazed Eggplant, a flavorful and satisfying dish with a delicious umami kick!

Japanese Chilled Tofu

Ingredients:

- **1 block silken tofu** (about 14 ounces or 400 grams)
- **2-3 tablespoons soy sauce**
- **1 tablespoon sesame oil**
- **1 teaspoon grated ginger**
- **1 tablespoon chopped green onions**
- **1 tablespoon bonito flakes** (optional)
- **1 tablespoon chopped fresh cilantro** or **shiso leaves** (optional)
- **1 teaspoon toasted sesame seeds** (optional)
- **1 small chili pepper**, thinly sliced (optional, for a touch of heat)

Instructions:

1. Prepare the Tofu:

- **Drain Tofu:** Carefully remove the tofu from its packaging and drain excess liquid. You can also wrap it in paper towels and gently press to remove additional moisture if needed.
- **Chill Tofu:** Place the tofu on a serving plate and refrigerate for at least 30 minutes to chill. This step enhances the flavor and texture of the tofu.

2. Prepare the Toppings:

- **Grate Ginger:** Peel and grate fresh ginger.
- **Chop Green Onions:** Thinly slice the green onions.
- **Prepare Optional Garnishes:** If using bonito flakes, cilantro or shiso leaves, sesame seeds, or chili pepper, prepare these as well.

3. Assemble the Dish:

- **Add Soy Sauce and Sesame Oil:** Drizzle the chilled tofu with soy sauce and sesame oil. You can adjust the amount of soy sauce based on your taste preferences.
- **Top with Garnishes:** Sprinkle the grated ginger, chopped green onions, and bonito flakes (if using) over the tofu. Add other optional garnishes such as cilantro, sesame seeds, or chili pepper if desired.

4. Serve:

- **Presentation:** Serve the Hiyayakko immediately after adding the toppings. It can be enjoyed as a light appetizer or side dish.

Tips:

- **Silken Tofu:** For the best results, use silken tofu as it has a smooth, creamy texture that works well with the cold serving method.
- **Garnish Options:** Feel free to customize the garnishes according to your preference. For a richer flavor, you can also add a drizzle of soy sauce or a sprinkle of sea salt.
- **Chilled Tofu:** Make sure the tofu is well-chilled before serving to enjoy the dish at its best.

Hiyayakko is a simple yet elegant dish that highlights the delicate flavor and texture of tofu, making it a refreshing addition to any meal. Enjoy!

Soba Noodle Salad

Ingredients:

For the Salad:

- **8 ounces soba noodles** (about 225 grams)
- **1 cup shredded carrots**
- **1 cup thinly sliced bell peppers** (red, yellow, or orange)
- **1 cup thinly sliced cucumbers**
- **1/2 cup edamame** (shelled, cooked)
- **1/4 cup chopped fresh cilantro** (or fresh mint or basil, if preferred)
- **1/4 cup sliced green onions**
- **1 tablespoon toasted sesame seeds** (optional)

For the Dressing:

- **1/4 cup soy sauce**
- **2 tablespoons rice vinegar**
- **1 tablespoon sesame oil**
- **1 tablespoon honey** or **sugar** (adjust to taste)
- **1 tablespoon grated ginger**
- **1 clove garlic**, minced
- **1 teaspoon sriracha** or **chili paste** (optional, for heat)

Instructions:

1. Cook the Soba Noodles:

- **Boil Water:** Bring a large pot of water to a boil.
- **Cook Noodles:** Add the soba noodles to the boiling water and cook according to the package instructions, usually for 4-5 minutes, until al dente.
- **Drain and Rinse:** Drain the noodles and rinse them under cold water to stop the cooking process and cool them down. Drain thoroughly and set aside.

2. Prepare the Vegetables:

- **Shred and Slice:** Shred the carrots, slice the bell peppers, and slice the cucumbers. If using frozen edamame, ensure they are cooked and cooled.

3. Make the Dressing:

- **Combine Ingredients:** In a small bowl or jar, whisk together the soy sauce, rice vinegar, sesame oil, honey (or sugar), grated ginger, minced garlic, and sriracha (if using) until well combined.

4. Assemble the Salad:

- **Combine Ingredients:** In a large bowl, combine the cooked soba noodles, shredded carrots, sliced bell peppers, sliced cucumbers, edamame, and chopped cilantro.
- **Add Dressing:** Pour the dressing over the salad and toss everything together until evenly coated.

5. Garnish and Serve:

- **Add Garnishes:** Sprinkle with sliced green onions and toasted sesame seeds if desired.
- **Serve:** Serve the salad immediately, or chill it in the refrigerator for about 30 minutes to let the flavors meld.

Tips:

- **Noodle Texture:** Be careful not to overcook the soba noodles; they should be firm and chewy, not mushy.
- **Vegetable Variations:** Feel free to add or substitute other vegetables such as snap peas, radishes, or avocado according to your preference.
- **Dressing Adjustments:** Adjust the sweetness or tanginess of the dressing by varying the amount of honey and rice vinegar to suit your taste.
- **Make Ahead:** This salad can be made ahead of time and stored in the refrigerator for up to 2 days. Just give it a good toss before serving.

Soba Noodle Salad is a versatile and nutritious dish that's both easy to prepare and deliciously satisfying. Enjoy this refreshing meal or side dish!

Grilled Salmon with Teriyaki Glaze

Ingredients:

For the Teriyaki Glaze:

- **1/4 cup soy sauce**
- **1/4 cup mirin** (sweet rice wine)
- **2 tablespoons brown sugar**
- **1 tablespoon honey** (or additional brown sugar)
- **1 tablespoon rice vinegar**
- **1 teaspoon sesame oil**
- **1 clove garlic**, minced
- **1 teaspoon grated ginger**
- **1 teaspoon cornstarch** (optional, for thickening)
- **1 tablespoon water** (if using cornstarch)

For the Salmon:

- **4 salmon fillets** (about 6 ounces each, skin-on or skinless)
- **Salt and pepper** (to taste)
- **1 tablespoon vegetable oil** (for grilling)
- **Sesame seeds** (for garnish, optional)
- **Chopped green onions** (for garnish, optional)

Instructions:

1. Prepare the Teriyaki Glaze:

- **Combine Ingredients:** In a small saucepan, combine the soy sauce, mirin, brown sugar, honey, rice vinegar, sesame oil, minced garlic, and grated ginger.
- **Simmer:** Bring the mixture to a simmer over medium heat, stirring occasionally until the sugar dissolves and the glaze starts to thicken (about 5-7 minutes).
- **Thicken (Optional):** If you want a thicker glaze, mix the cornstarch with water to form a slurry and stir it into the simmering sauce. Cook for an additional 1-2 minutes until the glaze is thickened. Remove from heat and let it cool.

2. Prepare the Salmon:

- **Season Salmon:** Pat the salmon fillets dry with paper towels. Season both sides with salt and pepper.
- **Preheat Grill:** Preheat your grill to medium-high heat. Brush the grill grates with vegetable oil to prevent sticking.

3. Grill the Salmon:

- **Grill Salmon:** Place the salmon fillets on the grill, skin-side down if they have skin. Grill for about 4-5 minutes per side, or until the salmon is cooked to your desired doneness and has nice grill marks. The internal temperature should reach 145°F (63°C) for fully cooked salmon.
- **Baste with Glaze:** During the last few minutes of grilling, brush the salmon with the teriyaki glaze to caramelize it slightly. Be careful not to burn the glaze.

4. Serve:

- **Plate the Salmon:** Remove the salmon from the grill and let it rest for a few minutes.
- **Garnish:** Drizzle additional teriyaki glaze over the salmon if desired. Garnish with sesame seeds and chopped green onions.

Tips:

- **Marinating:** For extra flavor, you can marinate the salmon in a small amount of the teriyaki glaze for 15-30 minutes before grilling.
- **Grill Temperature:** Make sure the grill is preheated to medium-high heat to get a good sear on the salmon.
- **Glaze Usage:** Save some of the teriyaki glaze to drizzle over the salmon after grilling, or serve it on the side for dipping.

Grilled Salmon with Teriyaki Glaze is a flavorful and satisfying dish that's both healthy and easy to prepare. Enjoy it with steamed rice and a side of vegetables for a complete meal!

Sweet Pea and Shrimp Tempura

Ingredients:

For the Tempura Batter:

- 1 cup all-purpose flour
- 1/2 cup cornstarch
- 1 teaspoon baking powder
- 1 large egg
- 1 cup cold sparkling water (or cold water)
- Ice cubes (to keep the batter cold)

For the Tempura:

- 8 large shrimp, peeled, deveined, and tails left on
- 1 cup sweet peas (fresh or frozen)
- Vegetable oil (for frying, such as canola or sunflower oil)

For Serving (Optional):

- **Tempura dipping sauce** (Tentsuyu) or soy sauce
- **Shredded daikon radish** (for garnish)
- **Lemon wedges** (for garnish)

Instructions:

1. Prepare the Ingredients:

- **Prep Shrimp:** Peel and devein the shrimp, leaving the tails on. Pat them dry with paper towels to ensure a crispy coating.
- **Prep Sweet Peas:** If using fresh sweet peas, rinse them and remove any tough fibers. If using frozen peas, thaw them and pat dry.

2. Make the Tempura Batter:

- **Combine Dry Ingredients:** In a large bowl, whisk together the flour, cornstarch, and baking powder.
- **Mix Wet Ingredients:** In another bowl, beat the egg lightly, then add the cold sparkling water.
- **Combine:** Pour the wet ingredients into the dry ingredients and stir gently. The batter should be lumpy and not overmixed. Adding ice cubes to the batter can help keep it cold, which is important for achieving a light and crispy texture.

3. Heat the Oil:

- **Preheat Oil:** In a deep skillet or pot, heat about 2 inches of vegetable oil to 350°F (175°C). Use a thermometer to monitor the temperature. If you don't have a thermometer, you can test the oil by dropping a small piece of bread into it; it should sizzle and turn golden.

4. Fry the Tempura:

- **Coat and Fry Shrimp:** Dip each shrimp into the tempura batter, allowing any excess to drip off. Carefully lower them into the hot oil. Fry in batches, making sure not to overcrowd the pan. Cook for about 2-3 minutes per side, or until golden and crispy. Remove with a slotted spoon and drain on a plate lined with paper towels.
- **Coat and Fry Sweet Peas:** Dip the sweet peas into the batter and fry in batches as well. Cook for 1-2 minutes until golden and crispy. Remove and drain on paper towels.

5. Serve:

- **Arrange Tempura:** Place the fried shrimp and sweet peas on a serving platter. Garnish with shredded daikon radish and lemon wedges if desired.
- **Serve with Dipping Sauce:** Serve with tempura dipping sauce (Tentsuyu) or soy sauce for dipping.

Tips:

- **Batter Temperature:** Keep the batter as cold as possible to ensure it remains light and crispy. Using sparkling water or ice-cold water helps with this.
- **Oil Temperature:** Maintain the oil temperature around 350°F (175°C) for the best results. If the oil is too hot, the tempura may burn; if it's too cool, it may become greasy.
- **Do Not Overmix:** Overmixing the batter can lead to a heavy coating. It's fine to have some lumps in the batter.

Sweet Pea and Shrimp Tempura is a delicious and elegant dish that's sure to impress your family and guests. Enjoy it fresh and crispy!

Green Tea Ice Cream

Ingredients:

- 1 cup whole milk
- 1 cup heavy cream
- 1/2 cup granulated sugar
- 3 tablespoons matcha powder (high-quality for best flavor)
- 4 large egg yolks
- 1/2 teaspoon vanilla extract (optional, for added depth)
- Pinch of salt

Instructions:

1. Prepare the Matcha Mixture:

- **Combine Matcha and Sugar:** In a medium bowl, whisk together the matcha powder and granulated sugar. This helps to evenly distribute the matcha and prevent clumps.

2. Heat the Milk and Cream:

- **Combine Milk and Cream:** In a medium saucepan, combine the whole milk and heavy cream. Heat over medium heat until just below boiling, stirring occasionally. Remove from heat.

3. Make the Matcha Mixture:

- **Mix Matcha with Milk:** Gradually add about 1/2 cup of the hot milk mixture to the matcha-sugar mixture, whisking continuously to form a smooth paste.
- **Combine with Remaining Milk:** Slowly whisk the matcha paste back into the saucepan with the remaining hot milk mixture.

4. Prepare the Custard Base:

- **Whisk Egg Yolks:** In a separate bowl, whisk the egg yolks until they are slightly thickened.
- **Temper the Eggs:** Gradually add about 1/2 cup of the hot milk mixture into the egg yolks, whisking constantly to temper the eggs.
- **Combine and Cook:** Pour the tempered egg yolk mixture back into the saucepan with the rest of the milk mixture. Cook over medium heat, stirring constantly with a wooden spoon or silicone spatula, until the mixture thickens and coats the back of the spoon (about 170-175°F or 77-80°C). Be careful not to let it boil.

5. Cool the Mixture:

- **Strain (Optional):** For a smoother texture, strain the mixture through a fine mesh sieve into a clean bowl to remove any lumps.
- **Cool:** Allow the custard base to cool slightly at room temperature, then cover and refrigerate until completely chilled (at least 4 hours or overnight).

6. Churn the Ice Cream:

- **Prepare Ice Cream Maker:** Follow the manufacturer's instructions for your ice cream maker.
- **Churn:** Pour the chilled custard base into the ice cream maker and churn until it reaches a soft-serve consistency (usually about 20-25 minutes).

7. Freeze:

- **Transfer to Container:** Transfer the churned ice cream to an airtight container.
- **Harden:** Freeze for at least 2 hours to firm up the ice cream before serving.

8. Serve:

- **Scoop and Enjoy:** Scoop the green tea ice cream into bowls or cones. Enjoy!

Tips:

- **Matcha Quality:** Use high-quality matcha powder for the best flavor and color. Culinary-grade matcha can be used but may not have the same depth of flavor as premium matcha.
- **Smooth Texture:** Straining the custard base helps ensure a smooth texture by removing any small bits of cooked egg or matcha clumps.
- **Chilling:** Be sure to chill the custard base thoroughly before churning to achieve the best texture.

Green Tea Ice Cream is a sophisticated and refreshing treat that offers a unique twist on classic ice cream. Enjoy the delicate balance of sweet and earthy flavors!

Fresh Edamame Beans

Ingredients:

- **1 pound fresh edamame beans** (in their pods)
- **Water** (for boiling)
- **Salt** (for seasoning)
- **Optional seasonings**: soy sauce, garlic powder, chili flakes, sesame seeds, etc.

Instructions:

1. Prepare the Edamame:

- **Rinse Beans:** Rinse the edamame beans under cold water to remove any dirt or debris.
- **Trim Pods (if needed):** If the edamame beans are still in their pods, there's no need to trim them. If they are shelled, ensure they are ready for cooking.

2. Cook the Edamame:

- **Boil Water:** Fill a large pot with water and bring it to a boil.
- **Add Salt:** Add a generous amount of salt to the boiling water (about 1-2 tablespoons), which will help season the beans.
- **Cook Edamame:** Add the edamame beans to the boiling water. Cook for 3-5 minutes if they are still in the pods or 1-2 minutes if they are shelled. The beans should be tender but still firm. Be careful not to overcook them as they can become mushy.

3. Drain and Season:

- **Drain Beans:** Drain the edamame beans in a colander and let them cool slightly.
- **Season:** While still warm, sprinkle additional salt over the edamame beans. You can also toss them with other seasonings like garlic powder, chili flakes, or a splash of soy sauce for extra flavor.

4. Serve:

- **Serving Options:** Serve the edamame beans warm or at room temperature. They can be enjoyed directly from the pods by squeezing the beans out with your fingers or teeth.

Tips:

- **Seasoning Variations:** Experiment with different seasonings to suit your taste. For a more Asian-inspired flavor, you can add a drizzle of sesame oil or sprinkle with toasted sesame seeds.
- **Serving:** Edamame can be served as a simple appetizer, added to salads, or used as a topping for various dishes.

- **Storage:** Cooked edamame can be stored in an airtight container in the refrigerator for up to 3 days. Reheat gently or enjoy cold.

Fresh edamame beans are a delicious, nutritious snack that is easy to prepare and customize to your taste preferences. Enjoy them on their own or incorporate them into your favorite recipes!

Japanese Cucumber Salad

Ingredients:

- 2 medium cucumbers
- 1/2 teaspoon salt
- 1/4 cup rice vinegar
- 1 tablespoon sugar (adjust to taste)
- 1 tablespoon soy sauce
- 1 teaspoon sesame oil
- 1/2 teaspoon sesame seeds (toasted, for garnish)
- 1 tablespoon chopped fresh cilantro or **shiso leaves** (optional, for garnish)
- 1/2 teaspoon **chili flakes** or **sliced fresh chili** (optional, for a bit of heat)

Instructions:

1. Prepare the Cucumbers:

- **Slice Cucumbers:** Thinly slice the cucumbers. You can use a mandoline for even slices or a knife if you prefer. Aim for paper-thin slices to ensure they are crisp and absorb the dressing well.
- **Salt the Cucumbers:** Place the cucumber slices in a colander or a bowl, sprinkle with salt, and let them sit for about 10 minutes. This process helps to draw out excess moisture and makes the cucumbers crisper.

2. Prepare the Dressing:

- **Mix Ingredients:** In a small bowl, combine the rice vinegar, sugar, soy sauce, and sesame oil. Stir until the sugar is completely dissolved. Adjust the sweetness or tanginess by adding more sugar or vinegar if desired.

3. Drain and Rinse Cucumbers:

- **Rinse Cucumbers:** After 10 minutes, rinse the cucumbers under cold water to remove excess salt. Pat them dry with paper towels or a clean kitchen towel to remove any remaining moisture.

4. Combine Salad:

- **Toss Salad:** Place the drained cucumber slices in a large bowl. Pour the dressing over the cucumbers and toss gently to coat all the slices evenly.
- **Marinate:** For best results, let the salad marinate for at least 10-15 minutes in the refrigerator. This allows the flavors to meld and the cucumbers to absorb the dressing.

5. Garnish and Serve:

- **Garnish:** Before serving, sprinkle the salad with toasted sesame seeds and chopped cilantro or shiso leaves if using. Add chili flakes or fresh chili slices for a touch of heat if desired.
- **Serve:** Serve chilled or at room temperature as a refreshing side dish or appetizer.

Tips:

- **Cucumber Types:** Japanese cucumbers are ideal for this salad due to their thin skin and mild flavor, but regular cucumbers work well too. If using regular cucumbers, you might want to peel them if the skin is tough.
- **Variations:** You can add other ingredients like thinly sliced radishes, shredded carrots, or seaweed for extra flavor and texture.
- **Make Ahead:** This salad can be made a few hours in advance and stored in the refrigerator. It's best enjoyed within 24 hours for the freshest taste and texture.

Japanese Cucumber Salad is a versatile and delightful dish that adds a crisp, tangy contrast to any meal. Enjoy its refreshing flavors!

Udon Noodles in a Light Broth

Ingredients:

For the Broth:

- **4 cups dashi stock** (you can use instant dashi powder mixed with water or homemade dashi)
- **1/4 cup soy sauce**
- **2 tablespoons mirin** (sweet rice wine)
- **1 tablespoon sake** (Japanese rice wine, optional)
- **1 teaspoon sugar** (optional, for a touch of sweetness)
- **1 clove garlic**, minced (optional, for extra flavor)
- **1 teaspoon grated ginger** (optional)

For the Udon Noodles:

- **8 ounces fresh udon noodles** (or dried udon noodles, if fresh is not available)
- **1 cup sliced mushrooms** (shiitake, enoki, or button mushrooms work well)
- **1 cup spinach** or **bok choy** (for added greens)
- **1/4 cup sliced green onions**
- **1/4 cup chopped nori** (seaweed) or **shredded dried bonito flakes** (katsuobushi) for garnish (optional)
- **1 tablespoon sesame seeds** (for garnish, optional)

Instructions:

1. Prepare the Broth:

- **Combine Ingredients:** In a large pot, combine the dashi stock, soy sauce, mirin, and sake. Add sugar if you like a touch of sweetness.
- **Simmer:** Bring the mixture to a gentle simmer over medium heat. If using garlic and ginger, add them to the pot. Simmer for about 5 minutes to allow the flavors to meld. Taste and adjust seasoning as needed.

2. Cook the Udon Noodles:

- **Boil Noodles:** If using dried udon noodles, cook them according to the package instructions. Fresh udon noodles usually need only a few minutes of boiling. Cook until just tender, then drain and rinse under cold water to stop the cooking process.
- **Add Noodles to Broth:** Add the cooked noodles to the simmering broth and heat through for 1-2 minutes.

3. Add Vegetables:

- **Add Mushrooms:** Add the sliced mushrooms to the broth and cook for a few minutes until they are tender.
- **Add Greens:** Add the spinach or bok choy and cook for another minute or until the greens are wilted.

4. Serve:

- **Dish Up:** Divide the noodles and vegetables among bowls. Ladle the hot broth over the noodles.
- **Garnish:** Garnish with sliced green onions, chopped nori, sesame seeds, or bonito flakes if desired.

Tips:

- **Dashi Stock:** If you can't find dashi, you can use chicken or vegetable broth as a substitute, though it will change the flavor slightly.
- **Vegetable Variations:** Feel free to add other vegetables like carrots, bell peppers, or bean sprouts based on your preference.
- **Seasoning:** Adjust the seasoning of the broth to your taste. You can add more soy sauce or mirin if you prefer a stronger flavor.

Udon Noodles in a Light Broth is a versatile and satisfying dish that's easy to make and can be customized with your favorite ingredients. Enjoy this comforting meal any time of year!

Smoked Salmon and Avocado Sushi

Ingredients:

For the Sushi:

- **2 cups sushi rice** (short-grain rice)
- **2 1/2 cups water**
- **1/4 cup rice vinegar**
- **2 tablespoons sugar**
- **1 teaspoon salt**
- **4 sheets nori** (seaweed)
- **4 ounces smoked salmon**, thinly sliced
- **1 ripe avocado**, sliced
- **1 cucumber**, peeled and julienned (optional)
- **Soy sauce**, for serving
- **Pickled ginger**, for serving
- **Wasabi**, for serving

For the Sushi Rice Seasoning:

- **1/4 cup rice vinegar**
- **2 tablespoons sugar**
- **1 teaspoon salt**

Instructions:

1. Prepare the Sushi Rice:

- **Rinse Rice:** Rinse the sushi rice under cold water until the water runs clear to remove excess starch. Drain.
- **Cook Rice:** In a rice cooker or pot, combine the rinsed rice and 2 1/2 cups of water. Cook according to the rice cooker instructions or bring to a boil, then reduce heat to low, cover, and simmer for 18-20 minutes until the rice is tender. Let it sit covered for 10 minutes after cooking.
- **Season Rice:** While the rice is cooking, combine 1/4 cup rice vinegar, 2 tablespoons sugar, and 1 teaspoon salt in a small saucepan over medium heat. Stir until the sugar and salt are dissolved. Do not boil. Let it cool.
- **Mix Rice and Seasoning:** Transfer the cooked rice to a large bowl. Gently fold the vinegar mixture into the rice using a wooden spoon or rice paddle. Let the rice cool to room temperature.

2. Prepare the Fillings:

- **Slice Ingredients:** Slice the smoked salmon and avocado. If using cucumber, julienne it into thin strips.

3. **Assemble the Sushi Rolls:**

    - **Prepare Nori:** Place a sheet of nori on a bamboo sushi mat lined with plastic wrap (for easy rolling).
    - **Spread Rice:** Wet your hands to prevent sticking and spread a thin layer of sushi rice evenly over the nori, leaving about 1 inch of nori at the top edge. Press the rice down gently but firmly.
    - **Add Fillings:** Lay slices of smoked salmon and avocado horizontally across the center of the rice. Add cucumber if using.
    - **Roll Sushi:** Carefully lift the bamboo mat and nori, rolling it over the fillings to form a tight log. Use the mat to shape and press the roll gently. Seal the edge of the nori by moistening it with a little water.
    - **Slice Roll:** Using a sharp knife, slice the roll into bite-sized pieces, cleaning the knife between cuts to ensure clean slices.

4. **Serve:**

    - **Plate:** Arrange the sushi rolls on a serving plate.
    - **Garnish and Accompaniments:** Serve with soy sauce, pickled ginger, and wasabi.

Tips:

- **Rice Temperature:** Ensure the sushi rice is at room temperature before assembling. Hot rice can make the nori soggy.
- **Cutting Rolls:** For clean cuts, use a sharp knife and wet it with water. This helps prevent sticking and crushing the rolls.
- **Customization:** Feel free to add other ingredients like cream cheese or thinly sliced scallions to the roll.

Smoked Salmon and Avocado Sushi is a delicious and elegant dish that's perfect for sushi lovers and those new to making sushi at home. Enjoy the creamy and smoky flavors in every bite!

Japanese Chive Pancakes (Negi Yaki)

Ingredients:

For the Pancakes:

- 1 cup all-purpose flour
- 1/2 cup dashi stock (or water)
- 1 large egg
- 1/2 teaspoon baking powder
- 1/2 teaspoon soy sauce
- 1/2 teaspoon sugar
- 1 cup chopped fresh chives (negi)
- 1/2 cup thinly sliced green onions (optional)
- Vegetable oil (for frying)

For the Dipping Sauce (Optional):

- 3 tablespoons soy sauce
- 2 tablespoons rice vinegar
- 1 teaspoon sugar
- 1 teaspoon sesame oil
- 1 teaspoon grated ginger (optional)
- 1 teaspoon sesame seeds (optional)

Instructions:

1. Prepare the Batter:

- **Mix Dry Ingredients:** In a large bowl, whisk together the flour and baking powder.
- **Combine Wet Ingredients:** In a separate bowl, whisk the dashi stock (or water), egg, soy sauce, and sugar until well combined.
- **Combine:** Gradually add the wet ingredients to the dry ingredients, stirring gently until just combined. The batter should be smooth but not overmixed.

2. Add Chives:

- **Incorporate Chives:** Fold the chopped chives and sliced green onions (if using) into the batter.

3. Cook the Pancakes:

- **Preheat Pan:** Heat a small amount of vegetable oil in a non-stick or cast-iron skillet over medium heat.
- **Cook Pancakes:** For each pancake, pour about 1/4 cup of batter into the hot pan and spread it out into a thin, even circle. Cook for about 2-3 minutes on each side, or until

golden brown and crispy. Flip carefully to cook the other side. Adjust the heat as necessary to avoid burning.

4. Prepare the Dipping Sauce (Optional):

- **Mix Sauce:** In a small bowl, combine soy sauce, rice vinegar, sugar, sesame oil, and grated ginger if using. Stir until the sugar is dissolved. Sprinkle with sesame seeds if desired.

5. Serve:

- **Plate:** Arrange the pancakes on a serving plate.
- **Serve with Sauce:** Serve the pancakes warm with the dipping sauce on the side, if using.

Tips:

- **Chives:** Fresh chives are best for this recipe, but you can also use green onions or scallions if chives are not available.
- **Consistency:** The batter should be thick enough to hold its shape but thin enough to spread easily in the pan.
- **Oil:** Ensure the oil is hot enough to create a crisp exterior but not so hot that it burns the pancakes.

Japanese Chive Pancakes (Negi Yaki) are a versatile and delicious dish that can be enjoyed as a quick snack, a part of a larger meal, or a tasty appetizer. Their savory flavor and crispy texture make them a delightful addition to any meal.

Cold Soba with Dipping Sauce

Ingredients:

For the Soba Noodles:

- **8 ounces soba noodles** (fresh or dried)
- **Water** (for boiling)

For the Dipping Sauce (Tsuyu):

- **1/2 cup soy sauce**
- **1/4 cup mirin** (sweet rice wine)
- **1/4 cup dashi stock** (or water if you prefer a lighter flavor)
- **1 tablespoon sugar** (optional, adjust to taste)

For Garnish (optional):

- **Thinly sliced green onions**
- **Grated daikon radish**
- **Wasabi**
- **Nori (seaweed) strips**
- **Sesame seeds**

Instructions:

1. Cook the Soba Noodles:

- **Boil Water:** Bring a large pot of water to a boil.
- **Cook Noodles:** Add the soba noodles and cook according to the package instructions, usually 4-6 minutes for dried noodles. Fresh soba noodles may cook faster, so check the package for specific times.
- **Drain and Rinse:** Drain the noodles and rinse them under cold running water to stop the cooking process and remove excess starch. This helps prevent the noodles from becoming sticky.

2. Prepare the Dipping Sauce:

- **Combine Ingredients:** In a small saucepan, combine soy sauce, mirin, dashi stock, and sugar if using.
- **Heat:** Heat the mixture over medium heat until it just begins to simmer. Stir to dissolve the sugar, if added.
- **Cool:** Remove from heat and let the sauce cool to room temperature. You can also chill it in the refrigerator if preferred.

3. Prepare Garnishes:

- **Slice and Grate:** Prepare any desired garnishes such as thinly sliced green onions, grated daikon radish, and nori strips.

4. Serve:

- **Arrange Noodles:** Place the chilled soba noodles on individual serving plates or bowls.
- **Serve with Sauce:** Pour the dipping sauce into small bowls for dipping.
- **Garnish:** Add optional garnishes to the noodles or serve them on the side.

Tips:

- **Soba Noodles:** If you're using dried soba noodles, be sure not to overcook them. They should be tender but still firm.
- **Dipping Sauce:** Adjust the strength of the dipping sauce by adding more or less dashi or water, depending on your taste preference.
- **Serving:** This dish is traditionally eaten by dipping the soba noodles into the sauce before each bite. This method keeps the noodles from becoming too soggy.

Cold Soba with Dipping Sauce is a light and satisfying dish that's perfect for a hot day or as a simple, elegant meal. Enjoy the combination of chilled noodles with a savory, umami-rich dipping sauce!

Soft-Boiled Egg with Soy Sauce

Ingredients:

- **4 large eggs**
- **1/4 cup soy sauce**
- **2 tablespoons mirin** (sweet rice wine)
- **2 tablespoons water**
- **1 tablespoon sugar**
- **1 clove garlic**, minced (optional)
- **1 teaspoon grated ginger** (optional)
- **1 tablespoon sesame oil** (optional, for extra flavor)
- **Green onions** or **nori** (seaweed) for garnish (optional)

Instructions:

1. Boil the Eggs:

- **Prepare Water:** Fill a saucepan with water, enough to cover the eggs by about an inch. Bring the water to a rolling boil.
- **Add Eggs:** Gently lower the eggs into the boiling water using a spoon or ladle to prevent cracking.
- **Boil:** Reduce the heat to medium and cook the eggs for 6-7 minutes for a soft, slightly runny yolk. Adjust the time if you prefer the yolk more set or less runny.
- **Cool Eggs:** Immediately transfer the eggs to a bowl of ice water or run them under cold water to stop the cooking process. Let them cool for a few minutes.

2. Prepare the Soy Sauce Marinade:

- **Combine Ingredients:** In a small bowl, mix together the soy sauce, mirin, water, and sugar. Stir until the sugar is completely dissolved.
- **Add Flavors (Optional):** If using garlic, ginger, or sesame oil, add them to the marinade.

3. Peel and Marinate the Eggs:

- **Peel Eggs:** Gently tap the cooled eggs on a hard surface to crack the shell, then peel them carefully.
- **Marinate:** Place the peeled eggs in a small container or bowl and pour the soy sauce marinade over them. Ensure the eggs are mostly submerged in the liquid. If needed, you can place a lid or cover the container to help the eggs marinate evenly.
- **Marinate Time:** Let the eggs marinate for at least 30 minutes. For a deeper flavor, you can refrigerate and let them marinate for up to 4 hours or overnight.

4. Serve:

- **Garnish (Optional):** Slice the marinated eggs in half and garnish with sliced green onions, nori strips, or a sprinkle of sesame seeds if desired.
- **Serve:** Enjoy the marinated eggs on their own, or use them as a topping for rice, noodles, or salads.

Tips:

- **Marinating:** The longer the eggs marinate, the more intense the flavor. Be careful not to marinate too long, as the soy sauce can become too salty.
- **Egg Texture:** Adjust boiling times slightly based on your preference for yolk consistency.
- **Storage:** Store marinated eggs in the refrigerator. They should be consumed within a week for the best quality.

Soft-Boiled Eggs with Soy Sauce are a flavorful and easy addition to many dishes, adding a rich umami flavor and a perfect soft texture. Enjoy!

Lotus Root and Carrot Stir-Fry

Ingredients:

- **1 medium lotus root** (about 8 ounces)
- **2 medium carrots**
- **1 tablespoon vegetable oil** (or any neutral oil)
- **2 cloves garlic**, minced
- **1 tablespoon ginger**, minced
- **2 tablespoons soy sauce**
- **1 tablespoon oyster sauce** (or vegetarian alternative)
- **1 tablespoon rice vinegar** or **white vinegar**
- **1 teaspoon sugar** (adjust to taste)
- **1/2 teaspoon sesame oil** (optional, for flavor)
- **1/4 cup water** or **vegetable broth**
- **1/4 cup sliced green onions** (for garnish)
- **1 tablespoon sesame seeds** (for garnish)
- **Red chili flakes** (optional, for heat)

Instructions:

1. Prepare the Lotus Root:

- **Peel:** Peel the lotus root with a vegetable peeler. You'll find a thin, brownish skin that should be removed.
- **Slice:** Cut the lotus root into thin slices, about 1/8 inch thick. You can cut them into rounds or half-moons depending on your preference.
- **Soak:** To prevent browning and remove excess starch, place the sliced lotus root in a bowl of water with a splash of vinegar or lemon juice. Soak for about 10 minutes, then drain and pat dry with a paper towel.

2. Prepare the Carrots:

- **Slice:** Peel the carrots and cut them into thin, matchstick-sized pieces or rounds, similar in size to the lotus root slices.

3. Cook the Stir-Fry:

- **Heat Oil:** Heat the vegetable oil in a large skillet or wok over medium-high heat.
- **Sauté Aromatics:** Add the minced garlic and ginger to the hot oil. Stir-fry for about 30 seconds until fragrant.
- **Add Vegetables:** Add the sliced lotus root and carrots to the skillet. Stir-fry for about 5-7 minutes, or until they start to become tender and slightly crispy.
- **Add Sauce:** In a small bowl, mix the soy sauce, oyster sauce, rice vinegar, and sugar. Pour the sauce over the vegetables.

- **Add Liquid:** Add the water or vegetable broth to the skillet. Stir well to combine and cook for an additional 2-3 minutes, or until the vegetables are fully cooked but still crisp-tender and the sauce has slightly thickened.
- **Finish:** Drizzle with sesame oil if using and give it a final toss.

4. Serve:

- **Garnish:** Transfer the stir-fry to a serving dish. Garnish with sliced green onions, sesame seeds, and red chili flakes if desired.
- **Enjoy:** Serve hot as a side dish or light main course.

Tips:

- **Lotus Root:** If you're not familiar with lotus root, it has a crunchy texture similar to water chestnuts and a slightly sweet, earthy flavor.
- **Vegetable Variations:** You can add other vegetables like bell peppers, snap peas, or mushrooms to the stir-fry for more variety.
- **Sauce Adjustments:** Adjust the sweetness, saltiness, and acidity of the sauce according to your taste preferences.

This **Lotus Root and Carrot Stir-Fry** is a delightful and healthy dish that showcases the unique texture of lotus root and the natural sweetness of carrots. Enjoy this crunchy and flavorful stir-fry!

Shoyu Ramen with Spring Vegetables

Ingredients:

For the Broth:

- 4 cups chicken or vegetable broth
- 1/4 cup soy sauce (shoyu)
- 2 tablespoons mirin (sweet rice wine)
- 1 tablespoon sake (optional, for added depth)
- 1 clove garlic, minced
- 1 teaspoon ginger, minced
- 1 tablespoon miso paste (optional, for extra umami)
- 1 teaspoon sesame oil

For the Ramen:

- 8 ounces fresh or dried ramen noodles
- 1 cup snap peas
- 1 cup asparagus, cut into 1-inch pieces
- 1/2 cup baby corn, halved if large
- 1/2 cup sliced shiitake mushrooms (or other mushrooms of choice)
- 1/2 cup thinly sliced carrots
- 2 green onions, sliced
- 1 tablespoon vegetable oil

Toppings (Optional):

- **Soft-boiled eggs** (recipe below)
- **Sliced bamboo shoots**
- **Nori (seaweed) sheets**
- **Chopped cilantro**
- **Sesame seeds**
- **Chili flakes** or **sriracha** (for heat)

Instructions:

1. Prepare the Broth:

- **Sauté Aromatics:** In a large pot, heat the sesame oil over medium heat. Add the minced garlic and ginger, and sauté until fragrant, about 1 minute.
- **Add Broth Ingredients:** Pour in the chicken or vegetable broth. Stir in the soy sauce, mirin, and sake (if using). Add miso paste if desired, stirring until it's fully dissolved.
- **Simmer:** Bring the broth to a gentle simmer and let it cook for about 10 minutes to allow the flavors to meld. Adjust seasoning to taste.

2. Prepare the Noodles:

- **Cook Noodles:** While the broth is simmering, cook the ramen noodles according to the package instructions. Fresh noodles typically cook faster than dried ones.
- **Drain:** Once cooked, drain the noodles and rinse under cold water to stop the cooking process. Set aside.

3. Cook the Spring Vegetables:

- **Sauté Vegetables:** In a separate pan, heat the vegetable oil over medium heat. Add the snap peas, asparagus, baby corn, mushrooms, and carrots. Stir-fry for about 3-5 minutes, or until the vegetables are tender-crisp and vibrant in color.
- **Season:** Season the vegetables with a pinch of salt and pepper.

4. Assemble the Ramen:

- **Combine Noodles and Broth:** Divide the cooked ramen noodles among serving bowls. Ladle the hot broth over the noodles.
- **Add Vegetables:** Top the ramen with the sautéed spring vegetables.
- **Garnish:** Add green onions and any additional toppings you prefer, such as soft-boiled eggs, bamboo shoots, nori, cilantro, sesame seeds, or chili flakes.

5. Prepare Soft-Boiled Eggs (Optional):

- **Boil Eggs:** Bring a pot of water to a boil. Gently add the eggs and cook for 6-7 minutes for a soft, runny yolk. Adjust cooking time for firmer yolks if desired.
- **Cool and Peel:** Transfer the eggs to an ice water bath to cool. Once cooled, peel the eggs and slice in half. Add to the ramen as a topping.

Tips:

- **Broth Variations:** Feel free to adjust the broth with additional ingredients like a dash of fish sauce or a bit of sesame paste for added flavor.
- **Vegetable Choices:** You can substitute or add other spring vegetables like baby bok choy, snow peas, or radishes based on what's in season.
- **Noodles:** Use fresh ramen noodles if possible for the best texture, but dried noodles work well too.

Shoyu Ramen with Spring Vegetables is a versatile and satisfying dish that celebrates the flavors of spring. Enjoy the harmony of tender noodles, savory broth, and crisp vegetables!

Pickled Cherry Blossoms

Ingredients:

- **1 cup cherry blossoms** (sakura), preferably from edible varieties
- **1/4 cup salt** (preferably sea salt)
- **1/2 cup ume vinegar** (or white vinegar as a substitute)
- **1/2 cup sugar** (optional, for a slightly sweet pickling)
- **1 tablespoon sake** (optional, for added depth of flavor)

Instructions:

1. Prepare Cherry Blossoms:

- **Wash Blossoms:** Gently rinse the cherry blossoms under cold water to remove any dirt or insects.
- **Dry:** Pat the blossoms dry with a paper towel or let them air dry completely.

2. Salt the Blossoms:

- **Layer with Salt:** In a bowl, layer the cherry blossoms with salt. Ensure they are well coated.
- **Massage:** Gently massage the salt into the blossoms to ensure even coating.
- **Weight:** Place a weight on top of the blossoms to help them release their moisture. You can use a small plate or a clean cloth with a weight on top.
- **Rest:** Let the blossoms sit for 1-2 hours at room temperature to allow them to release their moisture and wilt slightly.

3. Prepare Pickling Solution:

- **Combine Ingredients:** In a small saucepan, combine the ume vinegar (or white vinegar), sugar, and sake (if using). Stir until the sugar is completely dissolved.
- **Heat (Optional):** Heat the mixture over low heat to help dissolve the sugar, but do not boil. Allow it to cool completely.

4. Pickle the Blossoms:

- **Rinse Salt:** After the cherry blossoms have wilted, rinse off the excess salt under cold water and gently pat them dry with a paper towel.
- **Pack Jars:** Place the cherry blossoms into clean, sterilized jars, packing them lightly.
- **Pour Solution:** Pour the cooled pickling solution over the blossoms, ensuring they are fully submerged.
- **Seal Jars:** Seal the jars tightly with lids.

5. Pickling Time:

- **Refrigerate:** Store the jars in the refrigerator. The cherry blossoms will be ready to use in about 1-2 weeks. They can be kept for several months if stored properly.

Tips:

- **Choosing Blossoms:** Ensure you use edible cherry blossoms, as some varieties are ornamental and not suitable for consumption.
- **Substitute Vinegar:** If ume vinegar is not available, you can use rice vinegar or white vinegar, but ume vinegar gives a more authentic taste.
- **Sweetness:** Adjust the amount of sugar based on your preference for sweetness. You can also skip the sugar if you prefer a more savory pickle.

Pickled Cherry Blossoms are a delightful addition to dishes like rice, salads, or as a garnish for various Japanese recipes. Their delicate flavor and beautiful appearance make them a special ingredient to have on hand. Enjoy!

Daikon Radish Salad

Ingredients:

- **1 large daikon radish** (about 12 inches long)
- **1 medium carrot**
- **1/4 cup rice vinegar**
- **1 tablespoon soy sauce**
- **1 tablespoon sugar**
- **1 teaspoon sesame oil**
- **1 tablespoon sesame seeds** (toasted, for garnish)
- **2 green onions** (sliced)
- **1 tablespoon fresh cilantro** (chopped, optional)
- **1 small red chili** (sliced, optional, for a bit of heat)

Instructions:

1. Prepare the Vegetables:

- **Peel and Slice Daikon:** Peel the daikon radish and slice it into thin matchsticks or julienne strips. You can also use a mandoline for evenly sliced pieces.
- **Peel and Slice Carrot:** Peel the carrot and cut it into thin matchsticks or julienne strips, similar in size to the daikon radish.

2. Make the Dressing:

- **Combine Ingredients:** In a small bowl, whisk together the rice vinegar, soy sauce, sugar, and sesame oil until the sugar is dissolved and the dressing is well combined.

3. Toss the Salad:

- **Mix Vegetables and Dressing:** In a large bowl, combine the sliced daikon and carrot. Pour the dressing over the vegetables and toss well to coat evenly.
- **Add Garnishes:** Sprinkle the salad with toasted sesame seeds, sliced green onions, and fresh cilantro if using. Add sliced red chili for a touch of heat if desired.

4. Chill and Serve:

- **Chill (Optional):** Let the salad sit for about 10-15 minutes before serving to allow the flavors to meld. You can also refrigerate it for up to 30 minutes for a chilled salad.
- **Serve:** Serve the salad cold or at room temperature as a side dish or light meal.

Tips:

- **Texture:** For extra crunch, you can add other ingredients like thinly sliced cucumber or radish.
- **Sweetness:** Adjust the amount of sugar in the dressing to your taste. You can use honey or maple syrup as alternatives to granulated sugar.
- **Add Protein:** To make the salad more substantial, consider adding tofu cubes, shredded chicken, or edamame.

Daikon Radish Salad is a light, refreshing, and nutritious dish that pairs well with a variety of main courses. Its crisp texture and tangy dressing make it a perfect complement to any meal. Enjoy!

Japanese Potato Salad

Ingredients:

- **4 medium potatoes** (Yukon Gold or Russet work well)
- **1 medium carrot**
- **1/2 cucumber**
- **1/2 cup cooked ham** or **bacon** (optional, diced)
- **2 tablespoons rice vinegar**
- **1/2 cup Japanese mayonnaise** (such as Kewpie, or use regular mayonnaise)
- **1 tablespoon Dijon mustard** (optional, for extra flavor)
- **1 teaspoon sugar** (adjust to taste)
- **Salt and black pepper** (to taste)
- **2-3 green onions** (sliced, optional for garnish)
- **1 tablespoon chopped fresh parsley** (optional for garnish)

Instructions:

1. Prepare the Vegetables:

- **Peel and Dice Potatoes:** Peel the potatoes and cut them into 1-inch chunks. Place them in a pot and cover with cold water.
- **Cook Potatoes:** Bring to a boil over medium-high heat. Reduce heat and simmer until the potatoes are tender when pierced with a fork, about 10-12 minutes. Drain and let cool slightly.
- **Peel and Dice Carrot:** While the potatoes are cooking, peel the carrot and cut it into small cubes.
- **Cook Carrot:** In a small pot of boiling water, cook the carrot cubes for about 3-4 minutes until tender but still firm. Drain and let cool.
- **Slice Cucumber:** Thinly slice the cucumber and sprinkle with a little salt. Let it sit for about 5 minutes, then drain any excess moisture by pressing the slices between paper towels. You can also cut the cucumber into small cubes if preferred.

2. Prepare the Dressing:

- **Mix Dressing Ingredients:** In a large bowl, combine the mayonnaise, rice vinegar, Dijon mustard (if using), and sugar. Whisk until smooth. Adjust seasoning with salt and pepper to taste.

3. Combine Ingredients:

- **Mash Potatoes:** Once the potatoes are slightly cooled but still warm, roughly mash them with a fork or potato masher. You can leave some chunks for texture.
- **Mix Vegetables and Ham:** Add the diced carrots, cucumber, and ham (or bacon) to the bowl with the potatoes.

- **Add Dressing:** Pour the dressing over the potato mixture and gently fold until everything is evenly coated.

4. Chill and Serve:

- **Chill:** Cover the salad and refrigerate for at least 30 minutes to allow the flavors to meld. This also helps the salad firm up a bit.
- **Garnish:** Just before serving, you can garnish with sliced green onions and chopped parsley if desired.

Tips:

- **Mayonnaise:** Japanese mayonnaise is slightly sweeter and creamier than Western mayonnaise, but you can use regular mayonnaise if you prefer.
- **Texture:** For a creamier texture, mash the potatoes more thoroughly. For more texture, leave some chunks.
- **Add-ins:** Feel free to customize with other ingredients like boiled eggs, corn, or pickles.

Japanese Potato Salad is a versatile and comforting side dish that pairs well with many meals, from grilled meats to simple rice dishes. Enjoy the creamy, tangy, and slightly sweet flavors of this classic Japanese salad!

Tofu and Vegetable Stir-Fry

Ingredients:

- **14 ounces firm or extra-firm tofu** (drained and pressed)
- **2 tablespoons vegetable oil** (or any cooking oil of your choice)
- **1 bell pepper** (any color, sliced)
- **1 medium carrot** (sliced into thin rounds or matchsticks)
- **1 cup broccoli florets**
- **1 cup snap peas** (or snow peas)
- **1 small onion** (sliced)
- **2 cloves garlic** (minced)
- **1 tablespoon fresh ginger** (minced)
- **1/4 cup soy sauce** (or tamari for gluten-free)
- **2 tablespoons hoisin sauce** (optional, for added sweetness)
- **1 tablespoon rice vinegar** or **white vinegar**
- **1 tablespoon cornstarch** (mixed with 2 tablespoons water to make a slurry, for thickening)
- **1 teaspoon sesame oil** (optional, for flavor)
- **1 tablespoon sesame seeds** (for garnish, optional)
- **2 green onions** (sliced, for garnish, optional)

Instructions:

1. Prepare the Tofu:

- **Drain and Press:** Drain the tofu and press it to remove excess moisture. You can use a tofu press or wrap the tofu in a clean kitchen towel and place a heavy object on top.
- **Cube Tofu:** Cut the tofu into bite-sized cubes.

2. Cook the Tofu:

- **Heat Oil:** Heat 1 tablespoon of vegetable oil in a large skillet or wok over medium-high heat.
- **Sauté Tofu:** Add the cubed tofu and cook, turning occasionally, until all sides are golden and crispy, about 7-10 minutes. Remove the tofu from the skillet and set aside.

3. Stir-Fry Vegetables:

- **Add Oil:** In the same skillet, add the remaining tablespoon of vegetable oil.
- **Sauté Aromatics:** Add the minced garlic and ginger to the skillet and stir-fry for about 30 seconds until fragrant.
- **Add Vegetables:** Add the sliced bell pepper, carrot, broccoli florets, snap peas, and onion. Stir-fry for about 5-7 minutes, or until the vegetables are tender-crisp.

4. Combine Sauce and Tofu:

- **Mix Sauce:** In a small bowl, combine the soy sauce, hoisin sauce (if using), and rice vinegar.
- **Add Tofu and Sauce:** Return the cooked tofu to the skillet with the vegetables. Pour the sauce over the tofu and vegetables, stirring to coat evenly.
- **Thicken Sauce:** Add the cornstarch slurry to the skillet, stirring continuously until the sauce thickens and becomes glossy.

5. Finish and Serve:

- **Add Sesame Oil:** Drizzle the sesame oil over the stir-fry if using, and give it a final stir.
- **Garnish:** Sprinkle with sesame seeds and sliced green onions if desired.

6. Serve:

- **Serve Hot:** Serve the tofu and vegetable stir-fry over steamed rice, noodles, or as is for a low-carb option.

Tips:

- **Pressing Tofu:** Properly pressing the tofu helps it absorb flavors better and become crispy when cooked.
- **Vegetable Variations:** Feel free to use other vegetables like mushrooms, bok choy, or baby corn based on what you have available.
- **Spice It Up:** Add red pepper flakes or a splash of sriracha for a bit of heat.

This **Tofu and Vegetable Stir-Fry** is a versatile and satisfying dish that's perfect for a quick weeknight dinner or a healthy meal prep option. Enjoy the mix of crispy tofu and vibrant, flavorful vegetables!

Miso Soup with Asparagus

Ingredients:

- **4 cups dashi** (or vegetable broth as a substitute)
- **1/4 cup white or yellow miso paste** (adjust to taste)
- **1 cup asparagus** (cut into 1-inch pieces)
- **1/2 cup tofu** (firm or silken, cut into small cubes)
- **2 green onions** (sliced)
- **1 tablespoon soy sauce** (optional, for added depth)
- **1 teaspoon sesame oil** (optional, for flavor)
- **1/2 cup sliced mushrooms** (shiitake or button mushrooms, optional)
- **1 tablespoon wakame seaweed** (optional, rehydrated if dried)
- **1 clove garlic** (minced, optional, for extra flavor)
- **1 teaspoon fresh ginger** (minced, optional)

Instructions:

1. Prepare the Broth:

- **Heat Dashi:** In a large pot, heat the dashi (or vegetable broth) over medium heat until it begins to simmer. If using dashi granules or powder, follow the package instructions to prepare the broth.

2. Cook the Vegetables:

- **Add Asparagus:** Add the asparagus pieces to the simmering broth. Cook for about 3-4 minutes, or until the asparagus is tender but still crisp.
- **Add Tofu and Optional Ingredients:** If using, add the tofu cubes and sliced mushrooms to the pot. Cook for another 2-3 minutes, or until the tofu is heated through and the mushrooms are tender. If using wakame, add it now.

3. Prepare the Miso Paste:

- **Mix Miso:** In a small bowl, ladle a small amount of hot broth from the pot and whisk it with the miso paste until smooth and dissolved.
- **Add Miso to Soup:** Reduce the heat to low and stir the miso mixture back into the pot. Be careful not to boil the soup after adding the miso, as high heat can diminish its flavor.

4. Season and Garnish:

- **Adjust Seasoning:** Taste the soup and adjust the seasoning with soy sauce if needed. You can also add a teaspoon of sesame oil for extra depth of flavor if desired.
- **Add Green Onions:** Stir in the sliced green onions just before serving.

5. Serve:

- **Serve Hot:** Ladle the soup into bowls and serve hot. Enjoy the miso soup with asparagus as a comforting and flavorful dish.

Tips:

- **Miso Type:** White miso is milder and slightly sweeter, while yellow miso has a more robust flavor. Choose according to your taste preference.
- **Avoid Boiling:** Once miso is added, keep the soup at a gentle simmer to preserve the delicate flavors of the miso.
- **Vegetable Variations:** Feel free to add other vegetables like baby spinach, bok choy, or sliced radishes for added variety.

Miso Soup with Asparagus is a healthy, savory, and satisfying soup that highlights the umami-rich miso and the fresh crunch of asparagus. It's perfect for a light lunch or as a starter to a Japanese meal. Enjoy!

Sweet Potato Tempura

Ingredients:

- 2 medium sweet potatoes
- 1 cup all-purpose flour
- 1/2 cup cornstarch
- 1 teaspoon baking powder
- 1/2 teaspoon salt
- 1 large egg
- 1 cup ice-cold sparkling water (or cold water)
- **Vegetable oil** (for frying, such as canola or sunflower oil)

For Dipping Sauce (Tentsuyu):

- 1/2 cup dashi (or vegetable broth as a substitute)
- 2 tablespoons soy sauce
- 2 tablespoons mirin (sweet rice wine)
- 1 teaspoon sugar (optional, adjust to taste)

Instructions:

1. Prepare the Sweet Potatoes:

- **Peel and Slice:** Peel the sweet potatoes and slice them into 1/4-inch thick rounds or thin sticks.
- **Soak:** Place the sweet potato slices in a bowl of cold water for about 10 minutes to remove excess starch. This helps achieve a crispier texture. Drain and pat dry with paper towels.

2. Make the Tempura Batter:

- **Combine Dry Ingredients:** In a large bowl, whisk together the flour, cornstarch, baking powder, and salt.
- **Mix Wet Ingredients:** In a separate bowl, beat the egg and then mix in the ice-cold sparkling water.
- **Combine:** Pour the wet ingredients into the dry ingredients and stir gently until just combined. It's okay if the batter is a bit lumpy; overmixing can lead to a dense batter.

3. Prepare the Oil:

- **Heat Oil:** Pour vegetable oil into a deep fryer or large pot to a depth of about 2-3 inches. Heat the oil to 350-375°F (175-190°C). Use a thermometer to monitor the temperature for the best frying results.

4. Fry the Sweet Potatoes:

- **Coat Sweet Potatoes:** Dip the sweet potato slices into the tempura batter, allowing any excess to drip off.
- **Fry:** Carefully drop the battered sweet potato slices into the hot oil. Fry in batches, being careful not to overcrowd the pot. Cook for 2-4 minutes, or until the sweet potatoes are golden brown and crispy. Flip them halfway through if needed.
- **Drain:** Remove the tempura from the oil with a slotted spoon and drain on paper towels to remove excess oil.

5. Prepare the Dipping Sauce (Tentsuyu):

- **Combine Ingredients:** In a small saucepan, combine the dashi, soy sauce, mirin, and sugar. Heat over medium heat until the sugar dissolves and the mixture is warmed. Remove from heat and let cool slightly.

6. Serve:

- **Serve Hot:** Serve the sweet potato tempura hot with the dipping sauce on the side. You can also garnish with a sprinkle of sea salt or a squeeze of lemon juice if desired.

Tips:

- **Cold Batter:** The key to crispy tempura is using ice-cold water and not overmixing the batter. Cold batter helps create a light, airy texture.
- **Oil Temperature:** Maintain a consistent oil temperature to avoid greasy tempura. Too low, and the batter will absorb too much oil; too high, and the tempura will burn.
- **Batch Cooking:** Fry in small batches to keep the oil temperature steady and ensure even cooking.

Sweet Potato Tempura is a crispy, tender, and slightly sweet treat that's sure to be a hit. Whether served as an appetizer or a side dish, it's a delicious way to enjoy the unique flavor and texture of sweet potatoes. Enjoy!

Sushi Rolls with Seasonal Vegetables

Ingredients:

For the Sushi Rolls:

- **2 cups sushi rice** (short-grain or medium-grain)
- **2 1/2 cups water**
- **1/2 cup rice vinegar**
- **2 tablespoons sugar**
- **1 teaspoon salt**
- **Nori sheets** (seaweed sheets, cut into halves or quarters)
- **Seasonal vegetables** (such as cucumber, bell pepper, avocado, carrot, radish, or asparagus)
- **Soy sauce** (for dipping)
- **Pickled ginger** (for serving)
- **Wasabi** (optional, for serving)

Optional:

- **Cream cheese** or **hummus** (for a creamy texture)
- **Sesame seeds** (for garnish)

Instructions:

1. Prepare the Sushi Rice:

- **Rinse Rice:** Place the sushi rice in a sieve or fine-mesh strainer and rinse under cold water until the water runs clear. This helps remove excess starch.
- **Cook Rice:** In a rice cooker or pot, combine the rinsed rice and water. Cook according to the rice cooker instructions or bring to a boil, reduce heat to low, cover, and simmer for about 15 minutes until the water is absorbed and the rice is tender.
- **Season Rice:** While the rice is cooking, combine rice vinegar, sugar, and salt in a small saucepan. Heat over low heat until the sugar and salt are dissolved. Allow it to cool.
- **Mix Seasoning:** Transfer the cooked rice to a large bowl and gently fold in the vinegar mixture using a rice paddle or wooden spoon. Let the rice cool to room temperature.

2. Prepare the Vegetables:

- **Slice Vegetables:** Cut the vegetables into thin, long strips. For example:
  - **Cucumber:** Peel if desired, and cut into thin matchsticks.
  - **Bell Pepper:** Remove seeds and cut into thin strips.
  - **Carrot:** Peel and cut into matchsticks or use a julienne peeler.
  - **Avocado:** Cut into thin slices or strips.

3. Assemble the Sushi Rolls:

- **Prepare Nori:** Place a sheet of nori on a bamboo sushi mat lined with plastic wrap or parchment paper (shiny side down).
- **Spread Rice:** Wet your hands to prevent sticking, and spread a thin layer of sushi rice over the nori, leaving about 1 inch of nori at the top edge to seal the roll.
- **Add Fillings:** Lay the prepared vegetables in a line across the rice, near the bottom edge of the nori.
- **Roll:** Using the sushi mat, carefully lift the edge of the nori closest to you and begin rolling tightly, pressing gently to shape the roll. Use the exposed edge of the nori to seal the roll.
- **Slice Roll:** Use a sharp knife, lightly moistened to prevent sticking, to slice the roll into bite-sized pieces. Clean the knife between cuts for neat slices.

4. Serve:

- **Arrange:** Arrange the sushi rolls on a platter.
- **Garnish:** Garnish with sesame seeds if desired.
- **Accompaniments:** Serve with soy sauce, pickled ginger, and wasabi on the side.

Tips:

- **Rice Consistency:** Ensure the sushi rice is sticky but not too wet. If the rice is too dry, it will not stick together well.
- **Vegetable Variations:** Feel free to experiment with other seasonal vegetables or add ingredients like tofu or cooked mushrooms.
- **Rolling Technique:** Practice rolling tightly but gently to keep the fillings from spilling out and to achieve a uniform shape.

Sushi Rolls with Seasonal Vegetables are a fun and healthy way to enjoy sushi at home. The combination of fresh, crisp vegetables with seasoned rice and nori creates a delicious and satisfying meal. Enjoy making and eating your homemade sushi rolls!

Chilled Japanese Noodle Salad (Hiyashi Chuka)

Ingredients:

For the Noodles:

- **4 servings of ramen or soba noodles** (about 8 ounces)
- **Ice water** (for chilling the noodles)

For the Toppings:

- **1 medium cucumber** (julienned)
- **1 medium carrot** (julienned)
- **1/2 cup bean sprouts** (blanched if desired)
- **2-3 radishes** (sliced thinly)
- **2-3 slices of cooked ham** or **chashu pork** (cut into thin strips, optional)
- **2 eggs** (lightly beaten and cooked into a thin omelet, then sliced into strips)
- **1/4 cup corn kernels** (cooked or canned)
- **2 green onions** (sliced)
- **Sesame seeds** (for garnish, optional)

For the Dressing:

- **1/4 cup soy sauce**
- **2 tablespoons rice vinegar**
- **2 tablespoons sugar**
- **1 tablespoon sesame oil**
- **1 teaspoon mustard** (Japanese or Dijon, optional for a bit of heat)
- **1 clove garlic** (minced, optional)
- **1 teaspoon grated ginger** (optional)

Instructions:

1. Prepare the Noodles:

- **Cook Noodles:** Cook the ramen or soba noodles according to the package instructions. Drain and rinse under cold running water to cool them down and remove excess starch.
- **Chill:** Place the noodles in a bowl of ice water to chill thoroughly. Drain well before serving.

2. Prepare the Toppings:

- **Julienne Vegetables:** Julienne the cucumber and carrot. If using, slice the radishes thinly. If you prefer your bean sprouts blanched, briefly cook them in boiling water for 1-2 minutes, then rinse under cold water.

- **Prepare Eggs:** Make a thin omelet by heating a small amount of oil in a skillet, pouring in the beaten eggs, and cooking until just set. Allow it to cool, then roll it up and slice into thin strips.
- **Prepare Meat (Optional):** If using cooked ham or chashu pork, cut it into thin strips.

3. Make the Dressing:

- **Combine Ingredients:** In a bowl, whisk together the soy sauce, rice vinegar, sugar, sesame oil, mustard (if using), garlic, and ginger until the sugar is dissolved and the dressing is well combined.

4. Assemble the Salad:

- **Combine Ingredients:** Place the chilled noodles in a large serving bowl. Arrange the julienned cucumber, carrot, bean sprouts, radishes, corn, egg strips, and meat (if using) on top of the noodles.
- **Drizzle Dressing:** Pour the dressing over the salad just before serving, or serve the dressing on the side for guests to add according to their preference.
- **Garnish:** Garnish with sesame seeds and sliced green onions.

5. Serve:

- **Serve Cold:** Serve the Hiyashi Chuka chilled or at room temperature. Enjoy this refreshing and colorful salad as a light meal or a side dish.

Tips:

- **Noodle Alternatives:** While traditional Hiyashi Chuka uses ramen, you can also use soba noodles or even rice noodles for a gluten-free option.
- **Customization:** Feel free to add other ingredients such as sliced bell peppers, bamboo shoots, or even cooked chicken or tofu to suit your taste.
- **Make Ahead:** The dressing can be made ahead of time and stored in the refrigerator for up to a week. The salad can be assembled just before serving to keep the ingredients fresh and crisp.

Hiyashi Chuka is a delightful way to enjoy a variety of fresh vegetables and chilled noodles with a tangy, flavorful dressing. It's perfect for hot days or anytime you're looking for a light and satisfying meal. Enjoy!

Radish and Cucumber Pickles

Ingredients:

- **1 cup radishes** (sliced thinly or cut into thin rounds)
- **1 cup cucumber** (sliced thinly or cut into thin rounds)
- **1/2 cup rice vinegar**
- **1/4 cup water**
- **2 tablespoons sugar**
- **1 tablespoon salt**
- **1 tablespoon soy sauce** (optional, for extra depth of flavor)
- **1 teaspoon sesame seeds** (optional, for garnish)
- **1 teaspoon grated ginger** (optional, for added flavor)
- **1 small garlic clove** (sliced thinly, optional)

Instructions:

1. Prepare the Vegetables:

- **Slice Vegetables:** Wash and slice the radishes and cucumber into thin rounds or thin matchsticks, depending on your preference.
- **Salt Vegetables:** Place the sliced vegetables in a bowl and sprinkle with salt. Toss to coat evenly. Let sit for about 10 minutes to allow the salt to draw out excess moisture. This step helps the pickles stay crisp.

2. Prepare the Pickling Liquid:

- **Combine Ingredients:** In a small saucepan, combine the rice vinegar, water, sugar, and soy sauce (if using).
- **Heat Mixture:** Heat over medium heat, stirring occasionally, until the sugar is completely dissolved. Remove from heat and let cool slightly.

3. Combine and Pickle:

- **Rinse and Drain Vegetables:** After the vegetables have been salted and released some moisture, rinse them under cold water to remove excess salt. Drain well and pat dry with paper towels.
- **Add Flavorings (Optional):** If using, add the sliced garlic and grated ginger to the pickling liquid.
- **Pickle Vegetables:** Place the radish and cucumber slices in a clean jar or airtight container. Pour the cooled pickling liquid over the vegetables, making sure they are fully submerged.

4. Chill and Serve:

- **Refrigerate:** Seal the jar or container and refrigerate. The pickles will be ready to eat in about 1-2 hours, but they taste even better after a few hours or overnight as the flavors meld.
- **Garnish:** Before serving, you can sprinkle with sesame seeds if desired.

Tips:

- **Storage:** These pickles will keep in the refrigerator for about 1-2 weeks.
- **Customization:** Feel free to add other flavorings like red pepper flakes for heat, or a few sprigs of fresh dill for a different twist.
- **Texture:** For extra crispiness, you can also add a small amount of rice vinegar to the salt-coated vegetables before adding them to the jar.

Radish and Cucumber Pickles are a quick and refreshing side that adds a delightful crunch and tang to your meals. They're perfect for brightening up any dish with their vibrant color and crisp texture. Enjoy!

Spicy Tuna Tartare

Ingredients:

- **8 ounces sushi-grade tuna** (diced into small cubes)
- **1 avocado** (diced)
- **1 tablespoon soy sauce**
- **1 tablespoon sesame oil**
- **1 tablespoon sriracha sauce** (adjust to taste for heat)
- **1 teaspoon rice vinegar**
- **1 teaspoon honey** (or agave syrup)
- **1 teaspoon minced fresh ginger**
- **1 teaspoon minced garlic** (optional)
- **1 tablespoon chopped scallions** (plus extra for garnish)
- **1 tablespoon chopped cilantro** (for garnish)
- **1 tablespoon sesame seeds** (for garnish)
- **1 teaspoon lime juice** (optional, for extra brightness)

For Serving:

- **Tortilla chips, crackers,** or **toasted bread slices**
- **Pickled ginger** (optional)
- **Wasabi** (optional)

Instructions:

1. Prepare the Tuna:

- **Dice Tuna:** Cut the sushi-grade tuna into small, uniform cubes. Make sure the tuna is very fresh and of high quality.

2. Prepare the Spicy Sauce:

- **Combine Ingredients:** In a small bowl, mix together the soy sauce, sesame oil, sriracha sauce, rice vinegar, honey, minced ginger, and minced garlic (if using). Adjust the sriracha and honey to taste according to your preference for spiciness and sweetness.

3. Mix the Tartare:

- **Combine Tuna and Sauce:** In a mixing bowl, gently toss the diced tuna with the spicy sauce until the tuna is well coated.
- **Add Avocado:** Carefully fold in the diced avocado. Be gentle to avoid mashing the avocado.

4. Garnish and Serve:

- **Garnish:** Garnish with chopped scallions, cilantro, and sesame seeds.
- **Add Lime Juice:** Drizzle with lime juice if using, for an extra burst of freshness.
- **Serve:** Serve immediately with tortilla chips, crackers, or toasted bread slices on the side. You can also serve it on a bed of mixed greens or in small glasses for an elegant presentation.

Tips:

- **Sushi-Grade Tuna:** Ensure you use sushi-grade tuna for raw consumption. Freshness is key to the safety and flavor of this dish.
- **Adjust Spiciness:** Customize the level of spiciness by adjusting the amount of sriracha. For a milder version, use less sriracha or substitute with a milder chili sauce.
- **Make Ahead:** You can prepare the spicy sauce ahead of time and mix it with the tuna and avocado just before serving to maintain the freshness and texture.

Spicy Tuna Tartare is a vibrant and flavorful dish that's perfect for impressing guests or enjoying a special treat. Its combination of creamy avocado and spicy tuna makes it a delightful appetizer or light main course. Enjoy!

Green Tea Mochi

Ingredients:

- **1 cup glutinous rice flour** (also known as mochiko)
- **1/2 cup sugar**
- **1 cup water**
- **1 tablespoon matcha powder** (green tea powder)
- **Cornstarch or potato starch** (for dusting)
- **Red bean paste or sweetened bean paste** (optional, for filling)

Instructions:

1. Prepare the Mochi Dough:

- **Mix Dry Ingredients:** In a mixing bowl, combine the glutinous rice flour, sugar, and matcha powder. Mix well.
- **Add Water:** Gradually add the water to the dry ingredients, stirring continuously to avoid lumps. The mixture should be smooth and slightly thick.

2. Cook the Dough:

- **Steam Method (Traditional):** Pour the mochi mixture into a heatproof dish or bowl that fits into a steamer. Steam over simmering water for about 20-30 minutes, stirring occasionally, until the dough becomes translucent and thickens.
- **Microwave Method (Faster):** Transfer the mochi mixture to a microwave-safe bowl. Microwave on high for 1 minute, stir, then microwave for an additional 1 minute. Stir again, and microwave for a final 1-2 minutes, until the dough is thick and translucent.

3. Cool the Dough:

- **Let Cool:** Allow the mochi dough to cool slightly until it is comfortable to handle but still warm.

4. Shape the Mochi:

- **Prepare Work Surface:** Dust a clean surface or baking sheet with cornstarch or potato starch to prevent sticking.
- **Divide Dough:** Transfer the mochi dough onto the dusted surface. Lightly coat your hands with cornstarch to prevent sticking. Divide the dough into small, even pieces.
- **Shape Mochi:** Flatten each piece of dough into a small disk or round shape. If using, place a small spoonful of red bean paste in the center and fold the dough around it, pinching the edges to seal. Roll into a ball if desired.

5. Coat and Serve:

- **Coat:** Dust the shaped mochi with additional cornstarch or potato starch to prevent sticking and to give them a nice finish.
- **Serve:** Enjoy immediately or store in an airtight container at room temperature for up to 1-2 days. For longer storage, keep in the refrigerator but allow to come to room temperature before serving.

Tips:

- **Matcha Quality:** Use high-quality matcha powder for the best flavor and vibrant green color.
- **Avoid Overmixing:** Be careful not to overmix the mochi dough, as this can affect the texture.
- **Customization:** You can add other fillings like sweetened fruit or chocolate for a different twist.

Green Tea Mochi is a delightful treat that offers a unique combination of flavors and textures. Its chewy consistency and subtle matcha flavor make it a perfect dessert for any occasion. Enjoy making and eating this tasty Japanese delicacy!

Japanese Spring Vegetable Curry

Ingredients:

For the Curry:

- **1 tablespoon vegetable oil**
- **1 medium onion** (diced)
- **2 cloves garlic** (minced)
- **1 tablespoon fresh ginger** (minced)
- **2 medium carrots** (peeled and cut into bite-sized pieces)
- **1 cup potatoes** (peeled and cut into bite-sized pieces)
- **1 cup green beans** (trimmed and cut into 1-inch pieces)
- **1 cup asparagus** (cut into bite-sized pieces)
- **1 cup snap peas** (optional, trimmed)
- **1 medium zucchini** (cut into bite-sized pieces)
- **1 cup mushrooms** (sliced, optional)
- **3 cups vegetable broth** (or chicken broth)
- **1 large apple** (peeled and grated, for sweetness)
- **2 tablespoons soy sauce**
- **2 tablespoons Worcestershire sauce**
- **1 tablespoon curry powder** (adjust to taste)
- **1/2 teaspoon ground turmeric** (optional, for color)
- **1 tablespoon cornstarch** (mixed with 2 tablespoons water, for thickening)
- **Salt and pepper** (to taste)

For Serving:

- **Cooked white rice** (or brown rice)
- **Pickled ginger** (optional)
- **Chopped fresh cilantro** (optional, for garnish)

Instructions:

1. Prepare the Vegetables:

- **Cut and Dice:** Prepare all vegetables as described, cutting them into bite-sized pieces for even cooking.

2. Cook the Base:

- **Sauté Aromatics:** In a large pot or Dutch oven, heat the vegetable oil over medium heat. Add the diced onion and sauté until translucent, about 5 minutes.
- **Add Garlic and Ginger:** Stir in the minced garlic and ginger, cooking for another 1-2 minutes until fragrant.

3. Add Vegetables:

- **Cook Carrots and Potatoes:** Add the carrots and potatoes to the pot and cook for about 5 minutes, stirring occasionally.
- **Add Broth and Simmer:** Pour in the vegetable broth and bring to a boil. Reduce the heat to low, cover, and simmer for about 10 minutes or until the vegetables are just tender.

4. Add Remaining Vegetables:

- **Add Seasonal Vegetables:** Add the green beans, asparagus, snap peas, zucchini, and mushrooms (if using). Simmer uncovered for an additional 5-7 minutes, or until all vegetables are tender but still vibrant.

5. Season and Thicken:

- **Add Apple:** Stir in the grated apple, soy sauce, Worcestershire sauce, curry powder, and turmeric (if using). Adjust the seasoning with salt and pepper to taste.
- **Thicken Curry:** Mix the cornstarch with water to make a slurry and slowly stir it into the curry to thicken. Cook for a few more minutes until the sauce reaches your desired consistency.

6. Serve:

- **Serve with Rice:** Serve the curry hot over cooked white or brown rice. Garnish with pickled ginger and chopped fresh cilantro if desired.

Tips:

- **Customize Vegetables:** Feel free to use other spring vegetables such as baby corn, radishes, or peas depending on availability and preference.
- **Adjust Spice Level:** Japanese curry is usually mild, but you can adjust the heat by adding more curry powder or a bit of chili paste if you prefer a spicier dish.
- **Make Ahead:** This curry can be made ahead and stored in the refrigerator for up to 3-4 days. The flavors often improve after a day or two.

Japanese Spring Vegetable Curry is a versatile and comforting dish that celebrates the fresh flavors of spring. It's perfect for a hearty dinner and pairs beautifully with a bowl of rice. Enjoy the vibrant colors and rich, savory flavors of this seasonal curry!

Spinach Goma-ae (Spinach with Sesame Dressing)

Ingredients:

- **1 bunch fresh spinach** (about 8-10 ounces)
- **1 tablespoon sesame seeds** (white or black, for toasting)
- **1 tablespoon sesame paste** (tahini or Japanese *nerigoma* if available)
- **1 tablespoon soy sauce**
- **1 tablespoon mirin** (or honey as a substitute)
- **1 teaspoon sugar** (optional, for extra sweetness)
- **1 teaspoon rice vinegar** (or white vinegar)
- **1/2 teaspoon grated ginger** (optional, for extra flavor)
- **1 tablespoon water** (adjust as needed for consistency)

Instructions:

1. Prepare the Spinach:

- **Blanch Spinach:** Bring a large pot of water to a boil. Add the spinach and blanch for about 1 minute until wilted.
- **Cool Spinach:** Immediately transfer the spinach to a bowl of ice water to stop the cooking process and preserve the color. Let it cool for a few minutes.
- **Drain and Squeeze:** Drain the spinach well and squeeze out excess water by pressing it between your hands or using a clean kitchen towel.

2. Prepare the Sesame Dressing:

- **Toast Sesame Seeds:** In a dry skillet over medium heat, toast the sesame seeds until they are golden and fragrant, about 2-3 minutes. Let them cool slightly.
- **Grind Sesame Seeds:** Using a mortar and pestle or a spice grinder, grind the toasted sesame seeds into a coarse powder. Alternatively, you can use a food processor.
- **Mix Dressing:** In a bowl, combine the ground sesame seeds, sesame paste, soy sauce, mirin, sugar (if using), rice vinegar, and grated ginger (if using). Stir until well combined. Adjust the consistency with water as needed; the dressing should be creamy but pourable.

3. Combine Spinach and Dressing:

- **Cut Spinach:** Cut the spinach into bite-sized pieces if needed.
- **Toss:** Gently toss the spinach with the sesame dressing until evenly coated.

4. Serve:

- **Chill or Serve Immediately:** You can serve the Goma-ae immediately or chill it in the refrigerator for about 30 minutes to let the flavors meld.

- **Garnish:** Optionally, garnish with additional toasted sesame seeds or a sprinkle of sesame salt.

Tips:

- **Adjust Sweetness:** Depending on your preference, you can adjust the sweetness of the dressing by adding more or less sugar or mirin.
- **Make Ahead:** Goma-ae can be prepared ahead of time and stored in the refrigerator for up to 2-3 days. The flavor tends to develop more after resting.
- **Variations:** You can use other leafy greens like kale or bok choy in place of spinach, or add thinly sliced radishes for extra crunch.

Spinach Goma-ae is a refreshing and healthy side dish that pairs well with a variety of Japanese meals. The rich, nutty flavor of the sesame dressing complements the tender spinach beautifully. Enjoy this simple yet delicious dish as part of your next meal!

Strawberry Daifuku

Ingredients:

- **8-10 fresh strawberries** (hulled)
- **1 cup glutinous rice flour** (mochiko)
- **1/2 cup sugar**
- **3/4 cup water**
- **Cornstarch or potato starch** (for dusting and preventing sticking)
- **Red bean paste** (anko) (about 1/2 cup, optional, for filling)

Instructions:

1. Prepare the Strawberries:

- **Hull and Clean:** Wash and hull the strawberries. Pat them dry with a paper towel. If you're using red bean paste, form small balls of the paste that can wrap around the strawberries.

2. Prepare the Mochi Dough:

- **Mix Ingredients:** In a mixing bowl, combine the glutinous rice flour and sugar. Gradually add water while stirring to create a smooth batter.
- **Cook the Mochi Dough:**
    - **Steaming Method:** Pour the mixture into a heatproof dish and steam over simmering water for about 20-25 minutes, stirring occasionally, until the dough is translucent and thickened.
    - **Microwave Method:** Alternatively, you can microwave the mixture in a microwave-safe bowl. Microwave on high for 1 minute, stir, then microwave for an additional 1 minute. Stir again and microwave for 1-2 minutes more until the dough is thick and translucent.

3. Cool the Dough:

- **Let Cool:** Allow the mochi dough to cool slightly until it's comfortable to handle but still warm.

4. Shape the Daifuku:

- **Dust Work Surface:** Dust a clean surface or baking sheet with cornstarch or potato starch to prevent sticking.
- **Divide and Flatten:** Divide the mochi dough into small pieces, about the size of a golf ball. Flatten each piece into a small disk.
- **Wrap Strawberries:** If using red bean paste, place a strawberry on top of a disk of mochi dough and wrap the dough around it, pinching the edges to seal. If not using red

bean paste, you can simply wrap each strawberry with a piece of mochi dough, pinching the edges to seal.

5. Finish and Serve:

- **Coat with Starch:** Lightly coat each piece of daifuku with cornstarch or potato starch to prevent them from sticking together.
- **Serve:** Enjoy immediately or store in an airtight container at room temperature for up to 2 days.

Tips:

- **Fresh Strawberries:** Use firm, fresh strawberries that are not overly ripe to prevent them from getting mushy.
- **Moisture Control:** Be careful not to over-handle the mochi dough to keep it from becoming too sticky.
- **Red Bean Paste:** If you prefer, you can omit the red bean paste or use other fillings like sweetened cream cheese or fruit preserves.

Strawberry Daifuku is a fun and delightful dessert that pairs the chewy texture of mochi with the juicy sweetness of strawberries. It's perfect for a light and refreshing treat or for impressing guests with a beautiful and tasty Japanese confection. Enjoy making and eating this delightful treat!

Teriyaki Chicken with Seasonal Vegetables

Ingredients:

For the Teriyaki Chicken:

- **1 lb (450 g) boneless, skinless chicken thighs** (or breasts, if preferred)
- **1 tablespoon vegetable oil**
- **Salt and pepper** (to taste)

For the Teriyaki Sauce:

- **1/4 cup soy sauce**
- **1/4 cup mirin** (sweet rice wine) or **honey** (as a substitute)
- **2 tablespoons sugar**
- **1 tablespoon rice vinegar** (or white vinegar)
- **1 clove garlic** (minced)
- **1 teaspoon fresh ginger** (minced)
- **1 tablespoon cornstarch** (mixed with 2 tablespoons water, for thickening)

For the Vegetables:

- **1 cup broccoli florets**
- **1 cup bell peppers** (sliced, any color)
- **1 cup snap peas** (or green beans, trimmed)
- **1 medium carrot** (sliced thinly or julienned)
- **1 cup mushrooms** (sliced, optional)
- **1 tablespoon vegetable oil** (for sautéing vegetables)

For Serving:

- **Cooked rice** (white or brown)
- **Sesame seeds** (optional, for garnish)
- **Chopped scallions** (optional, for garnish)

Instructions:

1. Prepare the Teriyaki Sauce:

- **Combine Ingredients:** In a small saucepan, combine soy sauce, mirin (or honey), sugar, rice vinegar, minced garlic, and minced ginger.
- **Heat Mixture:** Bring to a simmer over medium heat, stirring occasionally until the sugar is dissolved.
- **Thicken Sauce:** Mix cornstarch with water to make a slurry and slowly stir it into the sauce. Cook for a few more minutes until the sauce thickens. Remove from heat and set aside.

2. Cook the Chicken:

- **Season Chicken:** Season the chicken thighs (or breasts) with salt and pepper.
- **Sear Chicken:** Heat vegetable oil in a large skillet or grill pan over medium-high heat. Add the chicken and cook for about 5-7 minutes per side, or until fully cooked and browned.
- **Glaze Chicken:** Once the chicken is cooked through, pour some of the teriyaki sauce over the chicken and continue to cook for another minute or two, until the sauce has caramelized slightly. Remove the chicken from the pan and let it rest for a few minutes before slicing.

3. Cook the Vegetables:

- **Heat Oil:** In the same skillet, add a bit more vegetable oil if needed.
- **Sauté Vegetables:** Add the vegetables (broccoli, bell peppers, snap peas, carrot, and mushrooms). Stir-fry over medium-high heat for about 5-7 minutes, or until the vegetables are tender-crisp.

4. Combine and Serve:

- **Slice Chicken:** Slice the cooked chicken into bite-sized pieces.
- **Toss Together:** Add the remaining teriyaki sauce to the vegetables and stir to coat. Add the sliced chicken and mix well.
- **Serve:** Serve the teriyaki chicken and vegetables over cooked rice. Garnish with sesame seeds and chopped scallions if desired.

Tips:

- **Custom Vegetables:** Feel free to use any seasonal vegetables you like or have on hand. Seasonal options might include zucchini, asparagus, or baby corn.
- **Marinate Chicken:** For extra flavor, you can marinate the chicken in some of the teriyaki sauce for 30 minutes to an hour before cooking.
- **Adjust Sweetness:** Adjust the sweetness of the teriyaki sauce according to your taste by adding more sugar or honey if needed.

Teriyaki Chicken with Seasonal Vegetables is a balanced and flavorful meal that's easy to prepare and perfect for a weeknight dinner. The combination of tender chicken, savory teriyaki sauce, and fresh vegetables makes it a crowd-pleaser that's sure to be enjoyed by everyone.

Miso-Glazed Grilled Eggplant

Ingredients:

- **2 medium eggplants** (Japanese or globe eggplants)
- **2 tablespoons vegetable oil** (for brushing)

For the Miso Glaze:

- **3 tablespoons white miso paste**
- **2 tablespoons soy sauce**
- **1 tablespoon mirin** (sweet rice wine)
- **1 tablespoon sugar** (or honey)
- **1 teaspoon sesame oil**
- **1 clove garlic** (minced)
- **1 teaspoon fresh ginger** (minced)

Instructions:

1. Prepare the Eggplants:

- **Slice Eggplants:** Slice the eggplants into 1/2-inch thick rounds. You can also cut them into halves or quarters lengthwise if you prefer larger pieces.
- **Salt the Eggplants:** Sprinkle the eggplant slices with salt and let them sit for about 20 minutes. This helps to draw out excess moisture and bitterness. Rinse and pat the eggplants dry with paper towels.

2. Prepare the Miso Glaze:

- **Combine Ingredients:** In a small bowl, whisk together the white miso paste, soy sauce, mirin, sugar (or honey), sesame oil, minced garlic, and minced ginger. Mix until smooth and well combined.

3. Grill the Eggplants:

- **Preheat Grill:** Preheat your grill to medium-high heat. You can also use a grill pan on the stovetop.
- **Brush with Oil:** Brush both sides of the eggplant slices with vegetable oil to prevent sticking.
- **Grill Eggplants:** Place the eggplant slices on the grill and cook for about 4-5 minutes per side, or until they are tender and have nice grill marks.

4. Apply the Miso Glaze:

- **Glaze the Eggplants:** During the last 2 minutes of grilling, brush the miso glaze over the eggplant slices. Let the glaze caramelize slightly on the grill.

5. Serve:

- **Garnish:** Remove the eggplants from the grill and transfer them to a serving plate. Optionally, sprinkle with sesame seeds, chopped scallions, or a drizzle of additional sesame oil for extra flavor.
- **Enjoy:** Serve warm as a side dish or over a bed of rice or noodles.

Tips:

- **Adjust Sweetness:** If you prefer a sweeter glaze, adjust the amount of sugar or honey to taste.
- **Miso Variety:** White miso is milder and sweeter, but you can use red or yellow miso for a stronger flavor.
- **Grilling:** Make sure to preheat the grill and oil the eggplants well to prevent them from sticking.

Miso-Glazed Grilled Eggplant is a flavorful and versatile dish that pairs wonderfully with a variety of meals. The rich miso glaze adds depth and complexity to the tender, smoky eggplant, making it a great addition to any Japanese-inspired meal. Enjoy!

Japanese Style Pancakes (Okonomiyaki)

Ingredients:

For the Pancake Batter:

- 1 cup all-purpose flour
- 1/2 cup **dashi stock** (or water as a substitute)
- 1 large egg
- 1 cup shredded cabbage
- 1/2 cup **grated carrot** (optional)
- 1/4 cup **chopped green onions**
- 1/4 cup **cooked bacon bits** or **diced ham** (optional)
- 1/4 cup **shredded cheese** (optional)
- **Salt and pepper** (to taste)

For Topping:

- **Okonomiyaki sauce** (store-bought or homemade, recipe below)
- **Japanese mayonnaise** (or regular mayonnaise)
- **Bonito flakes** (katsuobushi)
- **Aonori** (dried seaweed flakes, optional)
- **Pickled ginger** (beni shoga, optional)
- **Chopped green onions** (optional)

Homemade Okonomiyaki Sauce (if not using store-bought):

- 1/4 cup ketchup
- 2 tablespoons Worcestershire sauce
- 2 tablespoons soy sauce
- 1 tablespoon **mirin** (or honey as a substitute)
- 1 tablespoon sugar

Instructions:

1. Prepare the Okonomiyaki Sauce:

- **Mix Ingredients:** In a small bowl, combine ketchup, Worcestershire sauce, soy sauce, mirin (or honey), and sugar. Stir until well combined. Set aside.

2. Prepare the Batter:

- **Combine Ingredients:** In a large bowl, whisk together the flour and dashi stock (or water) until smooth. Add the egg and mix well.

- **Add Vegetables and Optional Ingredients:** Stir in the shredded cabbage, grated carrot (if using), green onions, bacon bits (if using), and shredded cheese (if using). Season with a pinch of salt and pepper.

3. Cook the Okonomiyaki:

- **Preheat Pan:** Heat a large non-stick skillet or griddle over medium heat. Lightly grease with oil.
- **Cook Pancake:** Pour a ladleful of batter into the pan and spread it out into a round shape about 1/2 inch thick. Cook for about 4-5 minutes, or until the bottom is golden brown and crispy.
- **Flip:** Carefully flip the pancake using a spatula and cook for an additional 3-4 minutes on the other side, or until cooked through and golden brown.

4. Add Toppings:

- **Apply Sauce and Mayonnaise:** Transfer the cooked okonomiyaki to a plate. Brush or drizzle with okonomiyaki sauce and Japanese mayonnaise.
- **Garnish:** Sprinkle with bonito flakes, aonori, pickled ginger, and chopped green onions if desired.

Tips:

- **Consistency:** The batter should be thick and able to hold the ingredients together but still pourable. Adjust with a bit more flour or liquid if needed.
- **Variations:** Feel free to add other ingredients like sliced mushrooms, shrimp, or even kimchi for different flavors.
- **Cooking Temperature:** Make sure the pan is properly preheated to ensure a crispy exterior while cooking the inside thoroughly.

Okonomiyaki is a fun and customizable dish perfect for a casual meal or for serving at gatherings. The combination of savory flavors and the ability to tailor the ingredients to your liking makes it a popular choice for many. Enjoy your homemade Japanese-style pancakes!

Chilled Edamame Salad

Ingredients:

For the Salad:

- **2 cups shelled edamame** (fresh or frozen)
- **1 cup cherry tomatoes** (halved)
- **1/2 cucumber** (diced or sliced)
- **1/4 red onion** (finely chopped)
- **1/4 cup fresh cilantro** (chopped, optional)
- **1/4 cup feta cheese** (crumbled, optional)
- **1/4 cup toasted sesame seeds** (optional, for garnish)

For the Dressing:

- **2 tablespoons soy sauce**
- **1 tablespoon rice vinegar**
- **1 tablespoon sesame oil**
- **1 tablespoon honey** (or maple syrup)
- **1 teaspoon grated fresh ginger** (or 1/2 teaspoon ground ginger)
- **1 clove garlic** (minced)
- **1 teaspoon toasted sesame seeds** (optional, for extra flavor)
- **Salt and pepper** (to taste)

Instructions:

1. Prepare the Edamame:

- **Cook Edamame:** If using frozen edamame, cook them according to the package instructions, usually by boiling for about 5 minutes until tender. If using fresh edamame, cook them in boiling water for about 3-4 minutes.
- **Cool:** Drain and rinse the edamame under cold water to cool them quickly and stop the cooking process. Set aside.

2. Prepare the Vegetables:

- **Chop and Dice:** While the edamame is cooling, prepare the cherry tomatoes, cucumber, and red onion.

3. Make the Dressing:

- **Combine Ingredients:** In a small bowl or jar, whisk together the soy sauce, rice vinegar, sesame oil, honey, grated ginger, minced garlic, and toasted sesame seeds (if using). Adjust seasoning with salt and pepper to taste.

4. Assemble the Salad:

- **Mix Ingredients:** In a large bowl, combine the cooked edamame, cherry tomatoes, cucumber, red onion, and cilantro (if using).
- **Add Dressing:** Pour the dressing over the salad and toss gently to combine.
- **Add Cheese and Seeds:** If using, sprinkle the crumbled feta cheese and toasted sesame seeds on top.

5. Chill and Serve:

- **Refrigerate:** Cover the salad and refrigerate for at least 30 minutes to allow the flavors to meld.
- **Serve:** Serve chilled as a refreshing side dish or light meal.

Tips:

- **Adjust Ingredients:** Feel free to add other vegetables like bell peppers, radishes, or avocado to the salad.
- **Make Ahead:** This salad can be made ahead of time and stored in the refrigerator for up to 3 days.
- **Season to Taste:** Adjust the amount of honey and soy sauce in the dressing to suit your taste preferences.

Chilled Edamame Salad is a versatile and healthy dish that's great for summer or any time you're in the mood for a cool, crisp salad. The combination of crunchy edamame and fresh vegetables with a tangy dressing makes it both satisfying and refreshing. Enjoy!

Shrimp and Vegetable Tempura

Ingredients:

For the Tempura Batter:

- **1 cup all-purpose flour**
- **1/2 cup cornstarch**
- **1 large egg**
- **1 cup ice-cold sparkling water** (or cold water)
- **1/2 teaspoon baking powder** (optional, for extra crispiness)
- **Pinch of salt**

For the Tempura:

- **12 large shrimp** (peeled and deveined, tails intact)
- **1 medium sweet potato** (sliced thinly)
- **1 cup broccoli florets**
- **1 medium carrot** (sliced thinly or julienned)
- **1 cup mushrooms** (shiitake or button, sliced)
- **Vegetable oil** (for frying)

For Serving:

- **Tempura dipping sauce** (tsuyu) or **soy sauce**
- **Grated daikon radish** (optional, for garnish)
- **Shredded nori** (optional, for garnish)

Instructions:

1. Prepare the Ingredients:

- **Prep Shrimp:** Peel and devein the shrimp, leaving the tails on. Pat them dry with paper towels to remove excess moisture.
- **Prep Vegetables:** Slice the sweet potato into thin rounds, slice the carrot, cut the broccoli into bite-sized florets, and slice the mushrooms.

2. Prepare the Tempura Batter:

- **Mix Dry Ingredients:** In a large bowl, whisk together the flour, cornstarch, and a pinch of salt.
- **Add Wet Ingredients:** In a separate bowl, beat the egg and add the ice-cold sparkling water (or cold water). Mix gently to combine.
- **Combine:** Pour the wet ingredients into the dry ingredients and stir gently until just combined. The batter should be lumpy; do not overmix. If using, fold in the baking powder for extra crispiness.

3. Heat the Oil:

- **Preheat Oil:** Heat vegetable oil in a deep fryer or large heavy-bottomed pot to 350°F (175°C). Ensure there is enough oil to fully submerge the tempura.

4. Fry the Tempura:

- **Coat Ingredients:** Dip the shrimp and vegetables into the tempura batter, allowing excess batter to drip off.
- **Fry:** Carefully lower the battered shrimp and vegetables into the hot oil. Fry in batches, being careful not to overcrowd the pot. Fry for 2-3 minutes, or until the tempura is golden brown and crispy.
- **Drain:** Remove the tempura from the oil using a slotted spoon and drain on paper towels.

5. Serve:

- **Arrange:** Arrange the tempura on a serving plate.
- **Garnish:** Optionally, garnish with grated daikon radish and shredded nori.
- **Dip:** Serve with tempura dipping sauce (tsuyu) or soy sauce.

Tips:

- **Cold Batter:** Keeping the batter cold is key to achieving a light and crispy texture. You can chill the batter in the refrigerator until you're ready to use it.
- **Oil Temperature:** Maintain a consistent oil temperature to ensure the tempura cooks evenly and stays crispy. Use a thermometer to monitor the temperature.
- **Batch Cooking:** Fry in small batches to avoid lowering the oil temperature and ensure each piece gets evenly cooked.

Shrimp and Vegetable Tempura is a delightful and versatile dish that can be enjoyed as an appetizer, side dish, or main course. The crispy, golden-brown coating and tender interior make it a favorite among tempura lovers. Enjoy your homemade tempura with a dipping sauce and your favorite accompaniments!

Japanese Beef and Vegetable Skewers (Kushikatsu)

Ingredients:

For the Skewers:

- **1 lb (450 g) beef sirloin** (or ribeye), cut into bite-sized pieces
- **1 red bell pepper** (cut into chunks)
- **1 green bell pepper** (cut into chunks)
- **1 medium onion** (cut into chunks)
- **1 zucchini** (sliced into rounds)
- **1 cup button mushrooms** (whole or halved)

For the Breading:

- **1 cup all-purpose flour**
- **2 large eggs**
- **1 1/2 cups panko breadcrumbs**
- **Vegetable oil** (for frying)

For the Dipping Sauce:

- **1/4 cup Worcestershire sauce**
- **2 tablespoons soy sauce**
- **1 tablespoon sugar**
- **1 tablespoon rice vinegar**
- **1 teaspoon grated fresh ginger**
- **1 clove garlic** (minced)

Instructions:

1. Prepare the Skewers:

- **Preheat Grill or Skillet:** Preheat your grill or a large skillet over medium-high heat. If using skewers, soak them in water for 30 minutes to prevent burning.
- **Assemble Skewers:** Thread the beef and vegetables onto the skewers, alternating between meat and vegetables.

2. Prepare the Breading Station:

- **Set Up Breading Station:** Place the flour in a shallow dish, beat the eggs in another shallow dish, and place the panko breadcrumbs in a third shallow dish.

3. Bread the Skewers:

- **Dredge in Flour:** Coat each skewer with flour, shaking off excess.

- **Dip in Egg:** Dip the floured skewer into the beaten eggs.
- **Coat with Panko:** Press the egg-coated skewer into the panko breadcrumbs, ensuring an even coating.

4. Fry the Skewers:

- **Heat Oil:** Pour vegetable oil into a large pan or deep fryer to a depth of about 2 inches. Heat to 350°F (175°C).
- **Fry Skewers:** Fry the skewers in batches, turning occasionally, until they are golden brown and cooked through, about 3-4 minutes per batch. Be sure not to overcrowd the pan.
- **Drain:** Remove from the oil and drain on paper towels.

5. Prepare the Dipping Sauce:

- **Combine Ingredients:** In a small bowl, whisk together the Worcestershire sauce, soy sauce, sugar, rice vinegar, grated ginger, and minced garlic. Stir until the sugar is dissolved.

6. Serve:

- **Arrange Skewers:** Arrange the cooked kushikatsu on a serving platter.
- **Serve with Sauce:** Serve with the dipping sauce on the side for dipping.

Tips:

- **Meat Tenderness:** Choose a tender cut of beef like sirloin or ribeye for the best results. Cut into uniform pieces for even cooking.
- **Breading:** Ensure each skewer is thoroughly coated in flour, egg, and panko for a crispy texture. Press the panko onto the skewer to help it adhere better.
- **Oil Temperature:** Maintain the oil temperature for crispy results. Use a thermometer to monitor the oil.

Kushikatsu is a versatile and fun dish that can be enjoyed with a variety of vegetables and dipping sauces. The crispy coating and juicy beef create a satisfying contrast that makes it a favorite at Japanese izakayas and a great addition to your homemade Japanese cuisine repertoire. Enjoy your homemade skewers!

Sweet Corn and Shrimp Croquettes

Ingredients:

For the Filling:

- **1 cup sweet corn kernels** (fresh or frozen)
- **1/2 lb (225 g) shrimp** (peeled, deveined, and finely chopped)
- **1 small onion** (finely chopped)
- **1 tablespoon vegetable oil**
- **1 tablespoon unsalted butter**
- **1 tablespoon all-purpose flour**
- **1/2 cup milk**
- **1/4 cup heavy cream**
- **Salt and pepper** (to taste)
- **1/4 teaspoon paprika** (optional)
- **1/4 teaspoon garlic powder** (optional)
- **1 tablespoon chopped fresh parsley** (optional)

For Breading and Frying:

- **1 cup all-purpose flour**
- **2 large eggs** (beaten)
- **1 1/2 cups panko breadcrumbs**
- **Vegetable oil** (for frying)

Instructions:

1. Prepare the Filling:

- **Cook Shrimp:** Heat 1 tablespoon of vegetable oil in a skillet over medium heat. Add the chopped shrimp and cook for about 2-3 minutes, or until pink and cooked through. Remove from the skillet and set aside.
- **Cook Onion and Corn:** In the same skillet, add 1 tablespoon of butter. Sauté the chopped onion until translucent, about 3-4 minutes. Add the sweet corn and cook for another 2 minutes. Remove from heat.
- **Make the Sauce:** In a medium saucepan, melt 1 tablespoon of butter over medium heat. Stir in the flour and cook for about 1 minute to form a roux. Gradually add the milk and heavy cream, whisking continuously until smooth and thickened. Season with salt, pepper, paprika, and garlic powder if using.
- **Combine Filling:** Add the cooked shrimp, onion, and corn to the sauce mixture. Stir in chopped parsley if desired. Cook for another 2 minutes until everything is well combined. Allow the mixture to cool slightly, then refrigerate for about 30 minutes to firm up.

2. Shape the Croquettes:

- **Form Patties:** Once the filling is chilled and firm, shape it into small oval or round patties, about 1-2 inches in diameter.

3. Bread the Croquettes:

- **Prepare Breading Stations:** Place the flour in a shallow dish, the beaten eggs in another dish, and the panko breadcrumbs in a third dish.
- **Coat Croquettes:** Dredge each croquette in flour, shaking off excess. Dip into the beaten eggs, then coat with panko breadcrumbs, pressing lightly to adhere.

4. Fry the Croquettes:

- **Heat Oil:** Heat about 2 inches of vegetable oil in a large pan or deep fryer to 350°F (175°C).
- **Fry Croquettes:** Fry the croquettes in batches, being careful not to overcrowd the pan, until they are golden brown and crispy, about 3-4 minutes per batch.
- **Drain:** Remove from oil using a slotted spoon and drain on paper towels.

5. Serve:

- **Arrange:** Place the croquettes on a serving plate.
- **Garnish:** Optionally, garnish with extra chopped parsley or a sprinkle of sea salt.
- **Enjoy:** Serve warm with dipping sauces such as ketchup, tonkatsu sauce, or a creamy dipping sauce.

Tips:

- **Cooling the Filling:** Ensure the filling is well-chilled before shaping to make it easier to handle and shape.
- **Frying in Batches:** Frying in small batches ensures even cooking and prevents the oil temperature from dropping too much.
- **Alternative Fillings:** You can customize the filling with other ingredients like mushrooms, cooked chicken, or different vegetables.

Sweet Corn and Shrimp Croquettes are crispy on the outside and creamy on the inside, making them a perfect appetizer or snack. They pair well with a variety of dipping sauces and are sure to be a hit at any gathering. Enjoy your homemade croquettes!

Grilled Asparagus with Soy Sauce

Ingredients:

- **1 bunch of asparagus** (about 1 pound, trimmed)
- **2 tablespoons soy sauce**
- **1 tablespoon olive oil** (or vegetable oil)
- **1 tablespoon rice vinegar** (or lemon juice)
- **1 tablespoon honey** (or maple syrup)
- **1 teaspoon sesame oil**
- **1 clove garlic** (minced, optional)
- **1/2 teaspoon freshly grated ginger** (optional)
- **1 tablespoon sesame seeds** (optional, for garnish)
- **Chopped green onions** (optional, for garnish)

Instructions:

1. Prepare the Asparagus:

- **Trim Asparagus:** Rinse the asparagus under cold water and trim the woody ends. You can do this by bending the asparagus gently until it snaps; the natural breaking point will remove the tough part.

2. Prepare the Marinade:

- **Combine Ingredients:** In a small bowl, whisk together the soy sauce, olive oil, rice vinegar, honey, sesame oil, minced garlic (if using), and freshly grated ginger (if using).

3. Marinate the Asparagus:

- **Marinate:** Place the asparagus in a large bowl or a resealable plastic bag. Pour the marinade over the asparagus and toss to coat evenly. Let it marinate for at least 15-30 minutes to absorb the flavors.

4. Preheat the Grill:

- **Heat Grill:** Preheat your grill to medium-high heat. You can also use a grill pan on the stovetop if you don't have access to an outdoor grill.

5. Grill the Asparagus:

- **Grill Asparagus:** Arrange the marinated asparagus on the grill in a single layer. Grill for about 4-6 minutes, turning occasionally, until the asparagus is tender and has nice grill marks. The grilling time may vary depending on the thickness of the asparagus.

6. Serve:

- **Garnish:** Transfer the grilled asparagus to a serving platter. Optionally, sprinkle with sesame seeds and chopped green onions for added flavor and texture.
- **Enjoy:** Serve warm as a side dish or light appetizer.

Tips:

- **Uniform Size:** Try to use asparagus stalks that are similar in size to ensure even cooking.
- **Grill Basket:** For smaller or thinner stalks, you might consider using a grill basket to prevent them from falling through the grates.
- **Check for Doneness:** The asparagus should be tender yet still crisp. You can test by piercing with a fork or knife.

Grilled Asparagus with Soy Sauce is a delightful and healthy side dish that complements a wide range of main courses. The combination of grilled flavor and savory marinade makes it a standout addition to any meal. Enjoy your grilled asparagus!

Japanese Sweet Potato and Chestnut Soup

Ingredients:

- **2 medium Japanese sweet potatoes** (or regular sweet potatoes), peeled and cubed
- **1 cup chestnuts** (fresh or pre-cooked and peeled; if using canned, drain and rinse)
- **1 small onion**, finely chopped
- **2 cloves garlic**, minced
- **1 tablespoon vegetable oil** (or olive oil)
- **4 cups vegetable broth** (or chicken broth)
- **1 cup coconut milk** (or heavy cream)
- **1 tablespoon soy sauce**
- **1 tablespoon miso paste** (white or yellow)
- **Salt and pepper** (to taste)
- **Chopped fresh chives** or **green onions** (for garnish, optional)
- **Toasted sesame seeds** (for garnish, optional)

Instructions:

1. Prepare the Ingredients:

- **Peel and Cube Sweet Potatoes:** Peel the sweet potatoes and cut them into cubes.
- **Prepare Chestnuts:** If using fresh chestnuts, score them with a knife and roast them in the oven at 400°F (200°C) for 20-25 minutes until the skins split. Peel the chestnuts once they are cool enough to handle. If using pre-cooked or canned chestnuts, simply chop them if they are large.

2. Cook the Aromatics:

- **Heat Oil:** In a large pot, heat the vegetable oil over medium heat.
- **Sauté Onion and Garlic:** Add the chopped onion and cook until it becomes translucent, about 3-4 minutes. Add the minced garlic and cook for an additional 1 minute until fragrant.

3. Cook the Sweet Potatoes and Chestnuts:

- **Add Ingredients:** Add the cubed sweet potatoes and chestnuts to the pot. Stir to combine with the onion and garlic.
- **Add Broth:** Pour in the vegetable broth, ensuring the sweet potatoes and chestnuts are covered. Bring to a boil, then reduce heat and simmer until the sweet potatoes are tender, about 15-20 minutes.

4. Blend the Soup:

- **Blend:** Use an immersion blender to puree the soup until smooth. If you don't have an immersion blender, you can carefully transfer the soup in batches to a regular blender. Blend until smooth and return to the pot.
- **Add Coconut Milk:** Stir in the coconut milk and return the soup to a gentle simmer.

5. Season the Soup:

- **Add Soy Sauce and Miso:** Stir in the soy sauce and miso paste until fully incorporated. Taste and adjust seasoning with salt and pepper if needed.
- **Simmer:** Let the soup simmer for an additional 5 minutes to allow the flavors to meld.

6. Serve:

- **Garnish:** Ladle the soup into bowls. Garnish with chopped fresh chives or green onions and toasted sesame seeds if desired.

Tips:

- **Texture:** Adjust the thickness of the soup by adding more broth or coconut milk if needed. If the soup is too thick, add a bit more liquid until you reach your desired consistency.
- **Miso Paste:** Miso adds depth of flavor to the soup, but if you don't have it, you can omit it or substitute with a bit of soy sauce or a touch of nutritional yeast for umami.
- **Chestnut Preparation:** If using fresh chestnuts, make sure to peel them thoroughly after roasting, as the skins can be quite tough.

Japanese Sweet Potato and Chestnut Soup is a delightful and warming soup that highlights the natural sweetness of the ingredients and provides a creamy, comforting texture. Enjoy this delicious soup as a starter or a light meal, perfect for cozy days!

Cherry Blossom Cake

Ingredients:

For the Cake:

- 1 1/2 cups all-purpose flour
- 1 cup granulated sugar
- 1/2 cup unsalted butter (room temperature)
- 1/2 cup milk
- 2 large eggs
- 1 teaspoon baking powder
- 1/2 teaspoon baking soda
- 1/4 teaspoon salt
- 1 teaspoon vanilla extract
- 1 tablespoon cherry blossom extract (or cherry extract, if available)
- 1/2 cup finely chopped candied cherries (optional)

For the Cherry Blossom Buttercream:

- 1 cup unsalted butter (room temperature)
- 3 cups powdered sugar
- 1/4 cup milk
- 1 teaspoon cherry blossom extract (or vanilla extract)
- **Pink food coloring** (optional)

For Decoration:

- **Edible cherry blossoms** (if available, for garnish)
- **Fresh cherries** (optional, for garnish)
- **Additional powdered sugar** (for dusting)

Instructions:

1. Prepare the Cake Batter:

- **Preheat Oven:** Preheat your oven to 350°F (175°C). Grease and flour two 8-inch round cake pans or line them with parchment paper.
- **Mix Dry Ingredients:** In a medium bowl, whisk together the flour, baking powder, baking soda, and salt.
- **Cream Butter and Sugar:** In a large bowl, cream the butter and granulated sugar together until light and fluffy using an electric mixer.
- **Add Eggs and Vanilla:** Beat in the eggs one at a time, then add the vanilla extract and cherry blossom extract.

- **Combine Wet and Dry:** Gradually add the dry ingredients to the wet ingredients, alternating with the milk, beginning and ending with the flour mixture. Mix until just combined.
- **Add Candied Cherries:** Gently fold in the finely chopped candied cherries, if using.

2. Bake the Cake:

- **Divide Batter:** Divide the batter evenly between the prepared cake pans.
- **Bake:** Bake in the preheated oven for 25-30 minutes, or until a toothpick inserted into the center comes out clean.
- **Cool:** Allow the cakes to cool in the pans for 10 minutes, then turn them out onto a wire rack to cool completely.

3. Prepare the Cherry Blossom Buttercream:

- **Beat Butter:** In a large bowl, beat the butter until creamy.
- **Add Powdered Sugar:** Gradually add the powdered sugar, beating well after each addition.
- **Add Milk and Extract:** Add the milk and cherry blossom extract (or vanilla extract) and beat until the frosting is light and fluffy. Adjust the consistency with more milk if needed.
- **Add Color:** If desired, add a few drops of pink food coloring and mix until you achieve the desired color.

4. Assemble the Cake:

- **Frosting:** Place one cake layer on a serving platter or cake stand. Spread a layer of buttercream frosting on top. Place the second cake layer on top and frost the top and sides of the cake with the remaining buttercream.

5. Decorate:

- **Garnish:** Decorate the cake with edible cherry blossoms, fresh cherries, or additional decorations of your choice. Lightly dust with powdered sugar if desired.

Tips:

- **Cherry Blossom Extract:** If cherry blossom extract is not available, you can substitute with cherry extract or a few drops of rose water for a floral note.
- **Cake Texture:** Ensure the cake layers are completely cooled before frosting to prevent the buttercream from melting.
- **Decoration:** Use edible flowers and fresh fruits to enhance the visual appeal of the cake.

Cherry Blossom Cake is a stunning and delicious way to celebrate the beauty of cherry blossoms. With its light, flavorful cake and elegant buttercream frosting, this dessert is perfect for special occasions or simply to enjoy a touch of springtime beauty. Enjoy your beautifully crafted cherry blossom cake!

Matcha Green Tea Cheesecake

Ingredients:

For the Crust:

- 1 1/2 cups graham cracker crumbs
- 1/4 cup granulated sugar
- 1/2 cup **unsalted butter** (melted)

For the Filling:

- 4 (8 oz each) packages **cream cheese** (room temperature)
- 1 cup granulated sugar
- 1 cup sour cream
- 1/2 cup heavy cream
- 3 large eggs
- 2 tablespoons **matcha green tea powder** (sifted)
- 1 teaspoon vanilla extract

For the Topping (optional):

- **Whipped cream** (for garnish)
- **Additional matcha powder** (for dusting)
- **Fresh berries** or **fruit** (for garnish)

Instructions:

1. Prepare the Crust:

- **Preheat Oven:** Preheat your oven to 325°F (160°C). Grease the sides of a 9-inch springform pan or line with parchment paper.
- **Mix Crust Ingredients:** In a medium bowl, combine graham cracker crumbs, granulated sugar, and melted butter. Stir until well combined and the mixture resembles wet sand.
- **Press into Pan:** Press the mixture evenly into the bottom of the prepared springform pan. Use the back of a spoon or the bottom of a glass to pack it down firmly.
- **Bake Crust:** Bake for 10 minutes, then remove from the oven and let it cool while you prepare the filling.

2. Prepare the Filling:

- **Beat Cream Cheese:** In a large bowl, beat the cream cheese until smooth and creamy using an electric mixer.
- **Add Sugar:** Gradually add the granulated sugar and continue beating until well combined.

- **Incorporate Matcha:** Add the sifted matcha powder and mix until evenly distributed. Ensure there are no lumps of matcha.
- **Add Eggs:** Beat in the eggs one at a time, mixing well after each addition. Scrape down the sides of the bowl as needed.
- **Add Sour Cream and Heavy Cream:** Mix in the sour cream, heavy cream, and vanilla extract until smooth and fully combined.

3. Bake the Cheesecake:

- **Prepare Pan:** Wrap the outside of the springform pan with aluminum foil to prevent water from seeping in if you are using a water bath.
- **Pour Filling:** Pour the cheesecake filling over the cooled crust in the springform pan.
- **Water Bath (Optional):** Place the springform pan in a larger baking dish and add hot water to the outer dish until it reaches halfway up the sides of the springform pan (this helps prevent cracking).
- **Bake:** Bake in the preheated oven for 60-70 minutes, or until the center is set but still slightly jiggly. The edges should be firm.
- **Cool:** Turn off the oven and let the cheesecake cool in the oven with the door slightly ajar for 1 hour. This helps prevent cracking. Afterward, transfer to the refrigerator and chill for at least 4 hours or overnight for best results.

4. Serve and Garnish:

- **Remove from Pan:** Once fully chilled, remove the cheesecake from the springform pan.
- **Garnish:** Optionally, top with whipped cream, a dusting of matcha powder, and fresh berries or fruit before serving.

Tips:

- **Matcha Quality:** Use high-quality matcha powder for the best flavor and color.
- **Smooth Texture:** Make sure to sift the matcha powder before adding it to the batter to avoid lumps.
- **Prevent Cracking:** A water bath helps to prevent the cheesecake from cracking by providing a moist environment. If you prefer not to use a water bath, make sure to bake at a lower temperature and monitor closely.

Matcha Green Tea Cheesecake is a sophisticated and delicious dessert that combines the creamy richness of cheesecake with the unique flavor of matcha. Its vibrant green color and subtle earthy notes make it a standout treat for any occasion. Enjoy your beautifully made cheesecake!